PEOPLE FOLLOW PEOPLE

PEOPLE FOLLOW PEOPLE

THE TWELVE CHARACTERISTICS OF AN INFLUENTIAL LEADER

SAM CAWTHORN

WILEY

First published in 2021 by John Wiley & Sons Australia, Ltd

42 McDougall St, Milton Qld 4064
Office also in Melbourne

Typeset in Warnock Pro 11/14pt

© John Wiley & Sons Australia, Ltd 2021

The moral rights of the author have been asserted

ISBN: 978-0-730-38855-5

A catalogue record for this book is available from the National Library of Australia

Cover design by Wiley

Printed in Singapore by Markono Print Media Pte Ltd

10 9 8 7 6 5 4 3 2 1

Disclaimer
The material in this publication is of the nature of general comment only, and does not represent professional advice. It is not intended to provide specific guidance for particular circumstances and it should not be relied on as the basis for any decision to take action or not take action on any matter which it covers. Readers should obtain professional advice where appropriate, before making any such decision. To the maximum extent permitted by law, the author and publisher disclaim all responsibility and liability to any person, arising directly or indirectly from any person taking or not taking action based on the information in this publication.

Also by Sam Cawthorn

Storyshowing: How to stand out from the storytellers

Bounce Forward: How to transform crisis into success

111 Tips to Bounce Forward

The Support Person (with Kate Cawthorn)

The 4 Needs 4 Teens: The teens guide for getting over it

The Positive Teen

The Bounce Theory

To my wife Kate, who has been my foundation and my rock.

To my three children, who help me each day to be a better father.

To our Global Teams, who are championing messages of thousands of Speakers all around the world.

CONTENTS

ABOUT THE AUTHOR

Since 2006, Sam Cawthorn has been sharing his personal story around the world. He has reached over 100 million people at live events, through his books and resources, and via social media.

Sam is a thought leader on peak performance and turnarounds, and a highly acclaimed professional speaking coach. He is the founder and CEO of Speakers Institute, an organisation dedicated to creating influencers with a powerful voice

in the marketplace. Today, Speakers Institute is a global company that boasts a team of more than 60 people and oversees more than 400 volunteers each year.

Early in his career Sam had carved out a niche as a youth futurist working for the Australian government. In October 2006, Sam's life changed forever when he was involved in a major car accident. Initially pronounced dead, he was eventually resuscitated, but his right arm had to be amputated and he was left with a permanent disability in his right leg.

During his recovery Sam chose not to return to his old job. Instead, he learned how to share his own story of 'bouncing forward' from his near-fatal injuries.

Sam has written seven previous books. *Bounce Forward* (2013) became an international bestseller. He has trained more than 5000 speakers around the world and has spoken in over 40 countries on some of the world's biggest stages.

ACKNOWLEDGEMENTS

I would like to acknowledge my writer, Bernadette Foley, who has been brilliant in extracting all of my wild, crazy ideas and distilling these into easily catchable messages.

I would also like to acknowledge my wife Kate, my three children and my Global Team who have been there every step of the way, helping our clients make a difference.

INTRODUCTION

How do you decide who to follow, who you will buy from, whose opinion you will respect, who you will learn from?

Do you base your decision on the number of likes or followers a person has on social media, or on how well known their brand is, or if they are famous and in the public spotlight? Or do you first seek to find out what that leader, influencer or teacher stands for — how they have chosen to contribute to the lives of the people around them, what they believe is important and what their values are? If this is the way you decide who you will follow, then it's probably also the way you want to lead and influence others. You want to become an influencer who stands for something, who will be there for people over the long term.

Do you want to change lives for the better, including your own, and to make a lasting difference? If so, you have the potential to be a leader and influencer others will choose to follow.

I believe this is the way many of us are now consciously deciding who we want to follow and whose influence we will accept. In recent years, and perhaps still today for some people, the idea of 'influencers' had negative connotations, bringing to mind social media celebrities doing makeup tutorials followed by millions on YouTube, the Kardashians on a reality TV show, Paris Hilton arriving at the latest party in a startlingly short dress, toned-up bodybuilders uploading photos of themselves, social media personalities aggressively promoting questionable advice. These really aren't the people who'll give the world a valuable and lasting legacy, are they?

The most important sources of influence, in my view, are increasingly individuals who are actually making a positive difference in the world — who encourage and empower others, whose opinions are progressive and inclusive, who stand up for diversity, who have the courage to call out inauthenticity and dishonesty, perhaps even challenging government or corporate unscrupulousness. Successful leaders and influencers, now and going forward, are those who are committed not only to making the world a better place, but to building strong character to lead others well.

In a decade that has started with the greatest upheaval in our lifetime, we want more from our influencers and decision-makers. Influence in the 2020s will be based on consciousness, progressive thinking, empathy, humanitarianism and strong character. We need leaders who will make a positive difference. And as leaders and influencers, this is what we should demand of ourselves. Whether in our own workplace or community, or in the wider marketplace, we want to invoke the power to successfully influence others and build trust in those in our sphere.

We want influencers and leaders who stand up for something beyond themselves, and we want to stand up for what we believe in.

What or who have we been following?

Have you ever felt that for too long we've been following organisations, governments, logos, brands and companies unquestioningly, that we've come to feel that these big names and organisations have too often let us down, that we can't always trust them and that they have no depth of character? People want to follow people, but they are looking for leaders who can clearly express what they believe in and show this through their actions. I see a shift building momentum, and the new era is all about what I call the profile economy.

When I was setting up my business, I started by building the product, the brand and the logo. But it wasn't quite working; I wasn't attracting enough people around me. It wasn't until I began to develop my profile that I started getting business, because people follow people. Potential clients first wanted to assess my character and what I believed in, and only then what I had to offer them.

Through this book, I will show how you can build your profile so you can successfully influence others, and become a leader people admire and respect. To win in the post-COVID world where influencers have so much power requires a focus on personal development, personal growth. The greatest way to build your profile as an influencer is to establish strong, lasting foundations.

Twelve seats at the table

Okay, that's easy to say, but how do you work out what your foundations are, or what they could be?

I like to use the metaphor of a table — a long table where you sit surrounded by your 12 most important attributes, beliefs and strengths. Chapter by chapter, we will explore each of these 12 seats or attributes. You can consider how they may fit into your life and how each might help you become an influencer who will be effective now and over the long term.

I grew up in country Tasmania as one of 11 children. With our parents we were a large family and at mealtimes we'd cram in around the kitchen table, all 13 of us at a table that was barely long enough to sit 12, but we all squashed in. Looking around at dinnertime, I'd see the people who meant so much to me. All these family members had their different personalities and characteristics. That image is one of the ways I visualise the idea of the 12 characteristics that has become so important in my life.

Looking around your table, you're not seeing big corporations, brands or political parties; you're seeing the faces of real people who matter to you. Think about individuals you know personally who you admire, leaders and influencers in your community or organisation who have inspired you. What makes them stand out as people worth following?

Let me introduce you to the 12 attributes sitting at my table and why I've chosen them above other possible alternatives.

Character before charisma

A lot of the time we follow people who have great charisma and engaging personalities, but I suggest we need to delve deeper to uncover what they believe in and stand for. We need to look at their character.

One time, early in my speaking career, I met someone who had amazing charisma; he was mesmerising and instantly won my full attention. Soon he had become my right-hand man and I was pushing him up on stage constantly as a speaker, and he was really good. I also spent a lot of time training and coaching him, and I was even considering handing over the reins to him to run the business for me. Unwisely, I hadn't looked beyond his impressive presentation to delve deeper into his character and what he actually stood for.

After about a year, I discovered my error the hard way when he set up his own company and tried to steal some of my clients. So right there I got burned. But looking back on that experience, I'm glad it happened. Because it taught me to screen the people I work with more closely. Charisma is a great trait that can take you a long way, but the first seat at my table always goes to Character.

Integrity before brand

Like charisma, brands can be appealing and capture our attention. If you want to succeed in business today, it's practically essential to build your own brand. However, brands are replaceable. They can quickly become outdated, then people lose interest and start looking for the next new thing. Integrity is a quality that lasts. Your own sense of integrity will be your guide in how to live, lead and influence authentically. Before building your brand, ask yourself what you stand for. What will you do to help others and why should others follow you? These days people look to leaders and influencers with integrity before they look to brands, even those that are traditionally trusted. Integrity, not a sparkling brand, has a seat at my table.

Vision before mission

We each need to define our big bold vision so we know where we're heading. Our vision is the thing that's waiting for us at the end of our journey. If it's very ambitious we may never reach it. Our mission gives us a guide to follow day by day, to ensure that every decision we make as leaders will be congruent with our values and vision. Both vision and mission are essential leadership tools, but Vision should always come first; mission follows.

Conscious before decision

We make thousands of decisions every day. Sometimes, whether in our personal life or in our business, we are faced with making a decision that could have huge outcomes. At that level especially, the decision-making process needs to start with being conscious of our values, our goals, the ways we want to convey the significance of what we can offer. Once we are conscious of all the implications, then we can examine the practicalities and finally make our choices. Conscious has an important seat at my table.

Completeness before purpose

Once you are sure of your values and are in alignment with your purpose, that positive feeling will stimulate and motivate you, making you a strong, appealing and compelling person to follow. You can't hope to achieve your purpose if you come to it feeling you're not good enough, or feeling frustrated or even angry. First find your sense of completeness, feel grateful for it and push on to fulfil your purpose. Give Completeness a seat at your table and you might find it life changing.

Trust before influence

Trust, or rather the lack of it, is a significant problem for big businesses, organisations and political parties these days. The major challenge for companies is to win the hearts and minds not only of their consumers but also of their employees. The most effective way to do this is for individuals to demonstrate through everything they do that they are trustworthy. Only then will they be able to influence others effectively. That is why Trust has a seat at my table.

Values before action

Actions are essential. Your days are filled with the actions you take based on the decisions you make — in the workplace and at home. But what happens when your actions lead you to the wrong place in your life, or when you're faced with a major decision and are not sure which way to go? What guides you as a leader and influencer that people want to follow? The answer is your values. It's your values that inform your actions. For that reason, Values occupies one of the 12 seats at my table.

Loyalty before opportunity

Everyone starting out in business needs to be open to new opportunities, some of which can lead to great things. As an entrepreneur myself, I love it when opportunities arise and I get to assess whether to seize them with both hands or to pass. But Opportunity doesn't have a seat at my table. I've given that seat to Loyalty. So often in life and your career you'll see how important it is to stay loyal to your vision, to your expertise, to your staff and mentors, and not to pass over them in order to chase the next new thing. There will be many times when you will benefit from staying loyal rather than running towards that shiny new opportunity.

Significance before success

Success is great. We celebrate successful people, look up to them and follow them. But success can crash overnight. Significance lasts. If we have made a positive impact on people's lives, we will always be significant to them, even after we're gone. I wish for your success, but my respect will be based on your significance. So Significance belongs at my table.

Small before big

In an era when the environment is crying out for our care, when millions of people have too little while a few have far too much, there are so many reasons why we should choose small before big. One is really practical: when we do the small things well, giving them our full attention, we often find they grow into something much bigger, something that has a major impact on our life or business. I celebrate Small and welcome it to my table.

Why before how

Whatever task we take on, we need to start by finding out *why* we need to do it. Only then can we work out *how* to do it. Our teams will come on board only once they understand why we are doing this. And when we can clearly articulate why we have to, need to or want to achieve something, then we can start to find different ways to do so. We can experiment with the *what* and *how* in our organisation or company, or in our own life. Why is one of the first things we should ask of ourselves and of others, so Why definitely has a seat at my table.

Story before data

We all want to make emotional connections with others. For better or worse, we think with our hearts as well as our brains, and to create these emotional ties there is nothing better than a story. We need precise data and comprehensive information too. You can't run a business or a country without knowing all the facts and figures; you need the analysis and the objective reasoning. But to trigger an emotional response, share a story. For me, Story rules supreme, so it always has a seat at my table.

Now look around at the 12 seats at your table and you'll see the support team you need if you're to be a successful leader today and in the future of influence.

It's your choice

It's up to you to choose how you'll fill the seats at your table and what priority you'll give to each one, and you need to choose wisely. Unfortunately, some people bring the wrong emotions, actions and traits to their table. Offence and anger definitely have no place there. Some people bring bad habits or addictions, some an insistence that they are not *good* or *worthy* enough. Some believe they are *not loved* or *don't belong* at the table, or simply don't know what to do there.

To help work out what you should focus on and what best suits your situation, seek advice from people you trust. At Speakers Institute I have an advisory board I rely on and trust. These are people who have achieved things I haven't done yet. They have attained a place in their career that I have yet to reach. Also, I have observed their character and how each of them work for others in their own businesses — how they respect people and live according to their own values. These people listen to me and we work together to decide which attributes, emotions and actions I should bring to my table and how I can use them every day.

When looking for your own mentors and advisers, ask these questions:

- Do they have experience and success in areas where you have yet to build experience?
- Is their character and integrity evident in their actions?
- Can you learn from and grow through them?
- Will they hold you accountable?

It's essential to be accountable to someone. So many people think they can become influencers on their own without actually being transparent or accountable to anyone else. That's not sustainable; we can't make real progress on our own. We all need someone to challenge us on what we believe in, to ask us why we are doing something or acting in a certain way. And to ask practical questions: Are we meeting our goals and targets? Are we treating our staff well? Are we leading successfully?

As a leader, you should inform and be informed

Leaders and influencers who attract loyal and lasting followers are people who are trustworthy and transparent and not afraid to share information.

Personally, I need and expect access to information to help me make judgements. Before reaching a decision, I first make sure I am fully informed. Then I find it really easy to draw a conclusion. In the past, I've based most of my big decisions on gut feel, but that's changing now that so many people rely on my decision making. As my company has grown, more people have come to depend on me at work. Our children rely on my wife, Kate, and me to make informed decisions. So even though I still find it easy to make decisions, these decisions now need to be a lot more conscious. And I need influencers around me who will tell me the truth, provide me with all the facts and figures I need, and prioritise my needs and the needs of my colleagues or family over their own interests.

Decisions about who I'll employ and who I'll work with must be based on having all the relevant information about those people. If this means talking to others who know them, even meeting them with their family to see them in a different environment, then that's what I'll do in order to make a conscious choice.

This is the style of leader and influencer I have chosen to be: honest, open, transparent and inclusive. It's not always easy or comfortable to share information, but it's essential to inform.

Leading to the future

I identify two major shifts in what people look for in the leaders and influencers they are prepared to follow today and going into the future.

One is that we're now looking to leaders who are part of what I regard as a beautiful push towards authenticity and transparency, even vulnerability. Think of the worldwide movement of ordinary people who are standing up and demanding that governments become more accountable and transparent, and that corporations be more open and trustworthy.

The other is that increasingly we aren't following organisations, governments, logos, products; rather, we are following other people.

Let's look at the three L's of leadership and influence:

- **Loyalty.** A good leader generates deep and sincere loyalty in his followers. A good leader will earn the loyalty and respect of their followers through what they do as well as what they say. They won't backstab such a leader or jump ship. They have that leader's back.

- **Longevity.** Leadership isn't just about being a leader or influencer once. Through the toughest times, a strong leader will push on with focus and determination. Their leadership will be characterised by consistency and longevity. It's about being there for the long term.

- **Legacy.** Great leaders, through that loyalty and longevity, will create a legacy that will last beyond their own career and even their own life. Their actions demonstrate that they place the interests of the people around them above their own. Leadership is not a title; it is something so much bigger.

If you aspire to become an outstanding leader, think about what you can offer others now and about what you would choose to be your legacy. Consider what will make you an influencer worth following, because ultimately *people follow people.*

Thank you for joining me on this journey to discover how to lead with purpose in the future of influence. Between the chapters that follow, three outstanding individuals who have also been my clients, Pauline Nguyen, Tony Tan and Fadzi Whande, share their stories to inspire and inform us, and I am grateful for their contributions. I hope their example will encourage you to share your own leadership stories with others.

MY LEADERSHIP JOURNEY

Like everyone, I fill many roles in my life. I'm a husband, a father and a brother, a speaker, an entrepreneur and a leader. I run a business, the Speakers Institute, that has grown in scale from a small startup to a very solid medium-sized company, and it's still growing. We have a big staff, a significant team of volunteers, and clients from all around Australia and the world.

When I started to think about leadership in the context of this book, I reflected on the people in my life who have shown me, through their example, how to lead others. They have been my mentors and taught me about running a business and leading teams, and what traits to value in myself and others.

Here I'm going to take you on a brief journey to introduce you to both my personal and my leadership story.

My first role models

Growing up in a large family in country Tasmania, I was number nine of 11 children. Looking back at my childhood, I can see that the first person who showed me how to lead was my father.

My father was an outstanding leader and a great role model for his sons and daughters. I looked up to him as someone who really stood up for what he believed in. He was a man of strong religious faith. He always held his ground; he spoke his mind when he needed to and kept quiet when he needed to. I don't remember him ever drinking alcohol, smoking or swearing. From a moral standpoint, he was a solid person, and that was something I aspired to; I was determined to follow his example. He set such high standards, though, that none of us really felt we could match them. I think many of us felt we couldn't meet his expectations, and this raised issues that each of us had to deal with.

Mum was amazing. She showed her love through acts of service and always provided for us. She didn't show a lot of affection, but she did the best she could with 11 children. She was not an easy person to live with when we were young, but she has since apologised to us all.

Witnessing the dynamics between my parents as we were growing up was interesting, to say the least. Yet the beautiful thing was that my parents were committed to each other and stayed together. As a couple they set an example that has taught me a lot about dealing with different personalities and finding common ground, even if the path to it can be rocky.

I also started to think about the various ways to lead by watching people in the many different churches we attended when I was a child and a teenager. I saw how what the church leaders, the pastors up the front, were saying and doing didn't always align with what they were telling us to do. I suppose my inner critic was strong and I was sometimes very judgemental of them. Holding up my father as the ultimate role model, I couldn't respect people who didn't live as he did and truly practise what they preached. This was something I thought a lot about as I got older and became a pastor myself.

The principal and some of the teachers at my school were leaders I admired. We went to a small public school in the country, where the staff really worked together. I saw little sign of gossiping between them; rather, the teachers supported each other and wanted the best for us kids.

As a young adult, my leadership mentor was Mr Moro, the general manager of the homewares store where I had my first full-time job; I stayed there for four years. With Mr Moro, you always knew he would look out for you and set a solid, ethical example. I respected him as a leader and aspired to match his strong moral principles.

My first leadership roles

My own first taste of leadership came when I became a kids' pastor in our church. I oversaw a couple of other people when we ran our kids' ministry and realised that I had to set an example for them too. Now *I* was the mentor. At the same time, I was asked to be the duty manager at Pizza Hut where I was working. I went on to run businesses and juggle everything that came with that role — looking after the finances, managing staff and stepping up to take decision-making responsibility. I was also overseeing people in my church. On top of all that, by then I was married and Kate and I had had our first child.

I was 23 and already on my leadership journey.

My first major leadership role came when I was working on a big theatre production. I had been asked to come along and do some dancing and singing in the show, but soon after rehearsals started the director bailed out after an argument with one of the other senior people in the crew. That meant the troupe of performers and stage crew were on their own, with no one to run the show. I was more than a little surprised when they voted for me to become the director, producer and choreographer.

There I was, at the ripe old age of 25, managing 30 people, most of whom were older than me, and running an entire theatre production. I was responsible for everything from negotiating with the venue to selling tickets and filling the concert hall, to overseeing the whole team. The production opened on cue and we had five sell-out performances.

At the start, shouldering that level of responsibility was overwhelming. Yet I was excited and really challenged by it too, and the fact that the project was a great success gave me the confidence to progress to other challenges.

Kate and I and our baby girl moved to Launceston, in the north of Tasmania. We went there mainly for my work, and also because I'd been given the opportunity to become second in charge in a church there, leading young people as a youth pastor. I was also working for Xerox selling photocopiers, though I have to say I wasn't too successful at that.

Then I got my job in job seeking — as a youth futurist.

At the time I was also teaching a number of adult education classes in singing and dancing. I had a strong singing and dancing career back in my twenties and I absolutely loved it. For a couple of years, I taught a 10-week course to classes of 20 to 30 people. It was great fun and offered a nice bit of extra cash on the side.

And that's when it happened. That almost fatal car crash would be a total life changer.

The turning point

I suppose I'd always known deep down that there was more for me to do in my life, and that I could make a real difference in many people's lives. As a result of the accident, I found something I never could have predicted. Through the experience I discovered a more fulfilling career through which I would ultimately touch many thousands of people.

At 26 years old, I was in the prime of my life, married, with two kids and a full-time job with the Australian federal government.

A big part of my job was travelling around the state so I had to drive a lot, which could be pretty tiring. That day, at around three in the afternoon, on the highway outside Devonport, I actually fell asleep at the wheel and veered over to the other side of the road. I later learned I was travelling at 104 km/h when I struck a semi-trailer going at 102 km/h head on, with a combined impact of 206 km/h. My car spun around into the path of another car behind the truck, which ploughed straight into my door.

The result can be imagined. A big part of my right arm was ripped off and the entire right side of my body was crushed, part of the car forced into the right side of my body. After about 18 minutes I lost consciousness. I was told later that by this time I had stopped breathing and my heart stopped beating for a couple of minutes. When the ambulance arrived the two paramedics managed to resuscitate me.

I was saved by the jaws of life. The paramedics cut me out of the car, stretchered me into the ambulance and raced for the hospital. I was on life support for a week. When I woke up and the doctors told me I'd lost my right arm above the elbow and I'd never be able to walk again, I first retreated into denial.

This couldn't have happened to me. It was a nightmare I convinced myself I'd soon wake up from. It was three days before I could accept this was actually my life and my reality. Then I went through a flood of emotions, always overshadowed by the thought of my kids growing up with a disabled father.

When I was out of hospital, a local youth group asked me to share my story, then I was approached by a school. I went on to share my story at school after school. Through my traumatic experience, it seemed like I had crashed into a new career path. I realised that this could be the beginnings of a new profession. I eventually decided to take the plunge, leave my job and learn how to market myself and my story.

This was the start of my journey towards building my profile and gaining recognition as a professional speaker.

Some years later, having travelled the world and presented in 40 countries, I met a couple of people who had great stories to share but didn't know how to communicate them. They came to me and said, 'Sam, it looks like you've made it. You've built your profile and you're making a living as a speaker. Can you teach us how to do it?' So I decided to share what I'd learned from my own experience with them, and within the next year or two they in turn became highly paid professional speakers.

It was then I realised that I had a formula I could teach to other people, showing them how to build their profile and become influencers in their space.

For the first four or five years of running the business, I was the only speaker and I had just one or two support staff. One day, during the period when I was completely focused on building the business and travelling the world as a professional speaker, Kate said to me, 'Enough is enough.'

I had just come through my busiest month ever, which included 56 flights, both domestic and international. By then we had three young kids and I wasn't at home much at all. I had to make a decision. Should I continue as a solopreneur on the professional speaking circuit, or should I look at actually running a business and teaching other people what I did in order for them to grow their profiles and influence in their industry?

Around this time, Google asked me to put on a workshop at their headquarters in Sydney. They wanted me to teach some of their leaders how to present and share stories. I asked them, 'Can we use your largest room and invite some of the public along to the seminar?' They said, 'Yeah, that would be fine.'

So they booked their biggest room, which sat 300 people, and I advertised it out there in the marketplace and more than 300 people signed up, including just a handful from Google. It was a sold-out event. I realised then that there was a huge demand out there for training in how to build a business profile, how to commercialise your voice and how to be an influencer.

That was the motivation I needed to set up Speakers Institute to teach others the skills behind becoming a successful speaker and a thought leader. Since then I've drawn on the wisdom of the best influencer trainers in the world, including body-language experts, publishers, media personalities, PR consultants, speaker bureaus and agents, as well as some of the best professional speaker trainers on the planet. I soaked up their knowledge in their areas of expertise, and in this way we built the Speakers Institute curriculum from the ground up.

As we developed, we became a premier training organisation, teaching our clients how to build their profiles in the new profile economy. Over the past five years, we've seen a really interesting transition as people previously influenced for the most part by governments, organisations, brands, products and logos have increasingly come to be influenced by people, individual human beings.

Learning to lead through life

Thinking about my life from my early childhood years on, I can see that I learned about leadership from many different sources and situations. It's probably the same for everyone. Think about the people who have been your mentors. Equally, there were probably people whose actions and conduct showed you how *not* to lead. We can learn from them too.

My leadership style is based primarily on encouragement. At Speakers Institute, we aim to encourage and empower people, and it all starts with the language we use. For example, when our opinion is sought, we start by offering positive reinforcement before putting forward our suggestions. We might advise, 'Be faithful with the small', or 'The best is yet to come', or 'It's time to shine.'

We truly believe in people, and we show this in both our words and our actions. This applies to everyone we come into contact with, especially our colleagues. We start every team meeting by acknowledging one another. We then talk about any incompletes and discuss ways to set them right, so we can all move on.

We lead and manage by taking into account the three greatest human fears: the fear of not being loved, the fear of not being good enough and the fear of not belonging. We find ways to overcome those fears so that we and the people around us can flourish.

Leading through growth

Thinking about how Speakers Institute has grown into a global company puts a big smile on my face. It makes me feel very content and fulfilled. I have a healthy work–life balance. I know a lot of people in a similar position to my own feel differently. Perhaps they feel guilty for not being there for their family because they're so busy building their business or travelling for work. I feel none of that, because I know I'm a good father and a loving husband. My wife and children are amazing, and that certainly helps me. I'm content with every aspect of my life, from my health and relationships through to my finances and the success of our business, and that gives me a deep sense of fulfilment.

So I'm certainly content, but I'm not satisfied.

Deep in my core, I know there's more — more opportunities to seize, more people to reach, more money to be made, more influence to wield, more lives that can be transformed, more to give. So no, I'm not satisfied, because I know there is so much more I can do as a leader.

This is a great motivator for all of us, in both our personal and professional life. Ask yourself, 'Am I content but not satisfied? Am I ready to do more, achieve more, have a positive impact on more people?'

I'm content but at the same time I'm hungry for more, because I have so much more to do.

Checking in with your mentors

For a leader or manager, it's a healthy practice to check in regularly with your mentors and with the people around you whom you respect. Be open to what they have to offer; it may not always be praise, but it's always certainly worth considering.

Kate, my life partner, is my anchor. She keeps me accountable and soon lets me know when my words and actions are misaligned in some way. And I have my oldest brother to confide in; I can talk to him when I feel really vulnerable, and share my highs and lows. I also have a pastor who helps me to realign when things feel a little out of control.

Professionally, I have my advisers on the Speakers Institute board as well as our leadership team. So I have a great range of people in my corner, people I can trust completely who will actively listen to me when I feel vulnerable or when things aren't going well.

My father was my first mentor and my benchmark. He would always help me to see what I should do, and I found his passing in 2017 incredibly difficult, to say the least. But I believe he's still there, and I carry with me what he taught me. His influence comes into my life every day.

Look to others when you need them

There came a time in my business when I realised that I wasn't learning from my failures as much as I should. That had a lot to do with my own arrogance and ego.

They say you can learn the easy way, the hard way or the tragic way. Learning the easy way, you learn from other people's mistakes. Learning the hard way, you learn from your own mistakes. But make sure you never choose the tragic way, which is when you don't learn from either. This is where I found myself when I started out in business as a speaker: I was failing but I wasn't necessarily learning from my mistakes; instead, I found myself failing again and again. That was when I realised how much I need people in my corner to keep me accountable.

I had to wake up to myself and say, 'Wait a second, I need people who are going to be there for me, to tell me the things I may not want to hear, but that I need to hear.' When I came to this recognition, I started to draw on my humility in order to become the person I knew I should be.

Finding that humility was not easy. I was a successful performer by that time, speaking to huge audiences around the world. I'd be a fool to imagine that I would remain unaffected by the ego and arrogance that so often follows success, unless I was aware of them and did something about them.

Never forget: confidence is a great asset, but arrogance can pull you down.

Yet there I was. Stepping off the stage after my speaking engagements, I would find people lining up to tell me how good I was, to get a photo with me, to ask for my autograph, to tell me that I'd changed their life, that I'd inspired them. Hearing that day in, day out, month in, month out, year in, year out — of course it affected me.

This is an issue for many people in positions of influence and leadership. You can be put on a pedestal. On social media people tell you 'you're amazing, awesome, inspiring'. Blah, blah, blah. Then you get one comment that says, 'You're ugly.'

That one comment breaks through, leaving you feeling stressed or anxious, and if such comments gain momentum you may find yourself descending into depression. All because one hurtful comment from one negative troll sets off a string of others.

As leaders and influencers, we need to build strong foundations for ourselves, for our business and for our colleagues. There will always be nay-sayers out there, but we have strategies to help us bounce forward from them. After all, if you can't draw the attention of the haters, you're clearly not making a big enough impact in the world.

Building these foundations has certainly helped me. Having people in my corner to tell me the things I need to hear, and not just the things that I want to hear, has kept me grounded.

If you want to grow as a leader, don't try to do it on your own. Reach out to mentors, study the good example of others.

If you have a bad experience, use the benefit of hindsight to make sure you do things differently next time. Trust and loyalty are a solid filter I use as I bring people into my sphere. These are two of the attributes I look for in the people around me, and I make a commitment to return them in kind.

CHAPTER ONE

CHARACTER
before charisma

Much of the time we follow people who are charismatic, people with big personalities. We enjoy being around them and hearing what they have to say. But I have found that having a big personality doesn't necessarily mean a person will grow as a leader and influencer, unless they have the strength of character to support them. Longevity as a leader and influencer requires character.

I have already mentioned an experience in the early days of my business when I met someone who had phenomenal charisma. I was so impressed with this guy. He knew just what to say to make me feel important and to convince me that the business I was setting up was a great idea. He was spellbinding and won my complete attention. Unfortunately, after doing business with him I discovered that he was also utterly dishonest. He had natural charisma, but no strength of character or respect for the truth, and I got burnt. This experience taught me that while charisma can be great, character and integrity are even more important.

Charisma

We are naturally drawn to charismatic people, attracted by their energy, their warmth and likability, even their looks and body language. They seem to say and do all the right things, and to know how to make the people around them feel special. Using all these appealing attributes, a charismatic person can easily influence others.

A charismatic person will have followers. After all, why wouldn't you want to spend time in the sphere of someone who is both attractive and makes you feel special? It's a good feeling, and a charismatic person can give you so much. They can draw on their attributes to lead and influence in a positive way. Think about some famous charismatic people in recent times. Take Barack and Michelle Obama, for example. In the White House and still today, they work to make the world a better place and they attract followers to their causes through their charisma and character. Charisma can be an incredibly positive attribute.

On the other hand, there are charismatic people who use this power solely for their own benefit. If they don't have integrity and a foundation that is truthful, then they won't help others and won't be positive leaders. Over time, the people around them will start to see through the illusions and self-serving behaviour and decide that they aren't really worth following.

As a leader and influencer, you should regularly check your own moral compass and ask, what standards am I setting for myself?

Do I speak up and act when my standards and values are threatened? Do I lead by example? In other words, do I show others the strength of my own character through what I do in every aspect of my life?

A good leader — whether a politician, a managing director, a teacher or an influencer — can use their own charisma to help them convey their message. That is a good thing and something we can all aim for. But if they want to be respected over the long term, they need to match their charisma with character.

Character

In his book *The Case for Character*, thought leader and bestselling author Michael McQueen 'highlights why character matters more than ever. In the coming years, consumers will demand ever-greater transparency, trustworthiness and values-alignment from the brands and businesses they engage with — a trend that leaders and organisations ignore at their peril'.

McQueen and I are on the same wavelength here. I believe that true character is even more appealing than charisma. As an influencer, a person of strong character who lives and leads honestly and ethically will outlast someone who is all about what they show us on the surface.

Character, for me, is a long-term game and is expressed through actions. Character means not giving up easily on relationships when things get tough. It means speaking truthfully, even when it's hard to do. It means standing up for what you believe in and not being a pushover. It means being true to your values even when others criticise or ridicule you for it.

It also means those around you trust you deeply, knowing you have their back and will never resort to backstabbing, gossiping or making negative comments about them. It is about having the courage to say what you really think. If you see or hear something you disagree with or you believe could hurt someone or harm your company or team, you call it out. That is strength of character.

Charisma is what we see, character is internal

For me, character is an internal quality. It's about looking deep within you and asking yourself, *Hey, is this what I believe in? Is this what I stand for? Is this my value system? Is this who I am?* Your actions and the way you live show your character.

Character is intrinsic to who you are and underpins your intentions. Charisma is external. It's what people see and hear. A charismatic person draws others to them by the attributes they show us. Charisma can be really positive. A charismatic person who also respects truth, has a strong character and works to improve people's lives, whether in the workplace, in the community or in their country, can be an outstanding leader. They can contribute so much to the people around them. Charisma can be wonderful, but character comes first; it is fundamental.

A strong character, being ready to stand up for the truth and for the best outcomes for the people around you, and charisma are a winning combination for a leader.

MICHELLE OBAMA AS INFLUENCER

Former First Lady Michelle Obama has become a major influencer over the past decade. She's a perfect example of an individual who has both strong character and great charisma.

The President of the United States arguably holds the most influential office in the world, which means the position of First Lady is also extremely important. Many of those who have fulfilled this role use their position to engage in philanthropy and do great work of their own. The First Lady is well placed to raise awareness about social issues. Recognising this, Michelle Obama worked hard to improve the lives of the people she and her husband served — in particular, women in the workforce and military families.

Her eight years as First Lady tell only a small part of her story. Michelle was an accomplished individual and influencer long before her husband attained America's highest office. Born in 1964, she enjoyed a distinguished career, graduating from Princeton University with *cum laude* honours in 1985. She also studied law at Harvard. It was while working with a Chicago-based law firm after leaving college that she met Barack Obama, and they married in 1992. She first came to national attention while standing by Barack's side when he was on the campaign trail to become a US senator.

In the years during and following her husband's presidency, Michelle revealed great charisma. She draws people to her with her warmth and her interest in them. She is also a person of great character who will speak out for what she believes in, even if others criticise her for doing so.

Her example shows that if you don't believe in yourself and your story, you won't persuade others to believe in you. To be an influencer, you need to stay true to your values.

(Continued)

5

No matter how charismatic you are, if you fake it your clients, audience or colleagues will see through it. The moment they sense a whiff of dishonesty, they disengage from your message. And you won't get those people back, because they don't trust you anymore.

Michelle Obama is such a powerful influencer because, as she puts it, 'I believe my story, I bring my truth, openness. I hear you and hug you — that's real. It shines through and it's not something you can hide.'

She doesn't hide anything about herself. She's open and transparent, which means she shares the good and the bad. Because of that, people trust her and are more likely to engage with her. She says, 'Authenticity means Michelle Obama is the same Michelle Obama you see here and with my girlfriends, walking the dog, being First Lady, it is the same person, and it's a lot easier because I don't have to pretend.'

Michelle Obama has long been an advocate for the advancement of women. She has a great passion for this cause, which she believes has come under direct attack in recent years. In one of her last speeches as First Lady, Michelle confronted these attacks directly:

'I listen to all of this and I feel it so personally, and I'm sure that many of you do too, particularly the women.

'The shameful comments about our bodies. The disrespect of our ambitions and intellect. The belief that you can do anything you want to a woman. It is cruel. It's frightening. And the truth is, it hurts.'

Here Michelle Obama does nothing to hide her anger, contempt and pain. Instead, she displays a searing passion for one of the causes closest to her heart.

It's this passion that encourages so many to connect with her on an emotional level. She shows people how attacks on women hurt even those in positions of high standing. In that sense, she relates her message to everyday people, and inspires and influences them.

> She connects with people because she fights for causes she truly believes in. Michelle Obama is authentic and passionate, charismatic and true to her character. She also understands how to get her message out to as wide an audience as possible. In addition, she has the ability to add depth to her story by linking her interests to her passion.

Can character and charisma be learned?

I believe strong character and charisma are innate. Some people are born with them. Michelle Obama, for example, is naturally charismatic and everything she does in her public life shows her strong, courageous character. However, I also think you can build your character by recognising what is important to you at the most fundamental level and by developing the courage to speak up, to defend your beliefs and to call out anything you believe to be untrue or unjust. Doing so requires a deep sense of purpose, and it may take time for you to recognise your own purpose. This doesn't necessarily mean you can learn how to develop a strong character, but you can strengthen the character you're born with. You can find a commitment and integrity within yourself that you can build on to become a stronger leader and influencer.

To some extent charisma can be learned by taking on board feedback about how you communicate. I don't believe that you can learn to be charismatic simply by watching and observing, though. You can only learn the qualities of charisma by interacting with others and receiving quality feedback about your interactions. And by doing so over and over again. The most useful feedback will be on first impressions, on how you communicate with others, how you show you're really listening to them and taking them seriously. You should welcome feedback on whether you show your excitement and passion for a project in a way that lets others feel it too.

Think about the energy you express. Is it positive? Does it exude charisma?

In my experience, it's easy to teach someone how to be excited and passionate when they communicate. It's much harder to teach someone how to follow their real truth. And that's character. We can teach the techniques, the secrets and the behavioural traits that are needed to appear charismatic. However, just because someone has learned how to develop their charisma, just because they're great up on stage as a speaker or when delivering an address in a board meeting, it doesn't necessarily mean they have character. You need both, and your character has to be genuine and come from within.

IN A NUTSHELL

Great leaders and influencers will attract people to them and their message through their charisma. Some people are born with an energy that draws people to them. Think of that old saying, 'You light up the room.' That is natural charisma. But if it doesn't come naturally, ask people around you to give you feedback on how you communicate, how you make them feel, whether they are persuaded that you really listen to them and make them feel special. Do you share your message with passion? These are aspects of charisma that you can learn and will need to learn if you want to be a great leader.

Even more important to the way you lead is that it is true to your character. Do you show strong values, ethical standards and integrity in your dealings with others, for example? Are you ready to stand up for what you believe in, even when you are the only one brave enough to do so? If others see you acting with courage and sincerity, with a commitment to improving your workplace, your community and your world, they will recognise the strength of your character. To be a great leader, be true to your character first; the charisma can follow.

CHAPTER TWO

INTEGRITY
before brand

In this book we're discussing brand in relation to human beings. We're not talking here about a product, a company logo, an organisation or a government, although they will all have their own brands, of course.

It's the human brand that will be the future of influence. You should look to building a big profile brand of yourself so you will be recognised, a visual brand that you are identified by, that becomes your trademark — think of the Pharrell hat, for example, or the Bono sunglasses or the Spanx red dress…

In fact, it's easy to build a visual brand so when your photos are posted online people will start to link your look to your name. If you do a Google search for Richard Branson, you will always see the beard, the long hair, and more often than not the covey of young women. The visual aspects of creating a brand are quite easy to catch.

A visual brand is a useful way to ensure you stand out from the crowd and gain recognition, but in itself it doesn't mean anything. A brand doesn't necessarily represent someone's true personality or character, or their integrity. You can build a brand through the consistency of the colours you wear, for instance, or of the content you release. However, if you don't back it up with integrity, authenticity and vulnerability, if you don't stand for something you truly believe is worthwhile, then your brand will eventually lose all value.

Your brand is important. It's what gets you in the door, what gets you past the gatekeepers. But it won't launch you into the stratosphere. It's the integrity of your character and actions that will propel you upward as a leader.

Your commitment and sincerity will drive you forward as an influencer. Your words and actions will show others that you are worth following.

Here are two questions I regularly ask myself: *Am I a leader worth following? Am I an influencer worth listening to?* If my brand is backed by integrity, then I am probably an influencer worth listening to and a leader worth following. If I have a great brand but I don't have the integrity to back it up, then I'm not really worth following.

Just as you can see a person's style and brand, there are visual aspects of integrity that you learn to recognise too. You'll see these signs in people who don't lose their cool in difficult situations, who stand up publicly for others, who support their staff and clients, who don't skip from relationship to relationship.

Will Smith has both a clever brand and true integrity. Following him on social media, you can see that he has created a unique brand with his goatee beard, amazing voice and vibrant personality. At the same time, I've never seen him lose his cool in public, swear or act up, or jump in and out of relationships. Look deeper than his brand and you'll quickly find evidence of his integrity. He does a lot of charity work, he's been in a long-term relationship for many years, and he's a good family man.

Bono is another great example of someone whose life is shaped by integrity before brand. We all recognise him by those signature glasses, but he also does a lot of work for charity organisations, much of it behind the scenes. Another celebrity, Angelina Jolie, acts and directs films in Hollywood while serving as a United Nations goodwill ambassador and dedicating much of her time to humanitarian causes; she is her own, globally recognised brand.

Your brand can be fun; it can bring you work and followers, and ensure you stand out from the crowd. It's good to carve out your own brand in your logo, your content — even your appearance — and your product. In business today, it's essential to give thought to your brand. Before considering what your brand will be, ask yourself what you stand for, how you will help others and why people should follow you.

The media in all its forms feeds the public's curiosity and can support a person's brand or pull them down.

As you rise in your career, ask yourself whether you behave differently when the cameras are turned off or when you're the only one left in the boardroom. A gauge of your integrity is how much you do for the good of your community or for the people you lead that no one or only a few people know about. A brand is on show; integrity can be strong even when it's in the shadows.

Of course, there are times when your integrity and character are out there for others to see, not ostentatiously but through your actions. People often identify a leader's integrity by observing how they interact with others, for example, by the way they talk about relationships or the opposite sex, or people of different social or ethnic backgrounds.

The quality of your followers

Given the huge number of likes and followers some big-name celebrities attract on social media, you might conclude that millions of people around the world are interested only in what's on the surface, what someone looks like rather than who they are and what they do. Instagram and TikTok, for example, are awash with people with follower numbers in the six figures whose brand hinges purely on what they look like — and those followers, for better or for worse, aren't that interested in integrity. They see brands in terms of entertainment rather than inspiring leadership, and that's fine.

For me and many others, though, it's less about the numbers than the quality of the followers. If your followers are engaged and influential and can help spread your positive message, or challenge you in a constructive way, or share their knowledge with you, then they are followers worth having.

Consider the question of age. Picking up on what integrity looks like in the way someone acts and lives their life is a learned skill that I believe increases as you get older. Most of those who follow a person's brand on social media are under the age of 30. These people haven't yet necessarily accrued the experience to distinguish integrity.

You can't fake integrity, which demands honesty, transparency, authenticity and conviction. You can't put on integrity as you would a hat. Integrity is an inside job!

It comes from deep within. You can learn all the marketing tactics for creating a brand and designing a visual presentation that makes you look good, but you can't fabricate integrity. Well, not in a way that can be sustained.

I heard of a man on the speakers' circuit who spends many hours producing videos and collecting photos of himself. When creating his videos he records one sentence, *stop*, then another sentence, *stop*, and another. Eventually, his editors splice together a video that makes him look and sound as if he is a powerful, leading influencer. When I met him I found he had no depth at all. This experience demonstrated to me that you can manufacture the 'look and feel' of integrity to a certain extent, but there will come a time when the façade will collapse and people will discover there's nothing behind it.

TIM FERRISS — A STRONG PERSONAL BRAND PLUS INTEGRITY

Leaders and influencers can have both a strong brand and integrity. You just have to be clear about what you believe in. Because, as I'll repeat a few times in this book to keep it in the front of your mind, if you don't stand for something, you'll fall for anything. Integrity has to come from a solid value system.

A great example of someone with an internationally known brand as well as a commitment to his personal values is Tim Ferriss. If you haven't heard of Tim, you've likely heard of his work. He's the author of *The 4-Hour Work Week*. He has also built on the 4-hour concept to create *The 4-Hour Body* and *The 4-Hour Chef*. It's fair to say that '4-Hour' is his business brand. But Ferriss is also an influencer who has established himself as a brand apart from his work. And much of his personal brand comes from the story behind the writing of his book.

Ferriss has achieved 'traditional' success in his life. A graduate of Princeton University, he began working for a start-up in Silicon Valley. The job didn't work out, as Ferriss

(Continued)

found himself frustrated by how much work he did for so little pay. So he decided to create a supplements company called BodyQUICK.

The venture took off and Ferriss soon found himself at the helm of a rapidly growing company. Unfortunately, this meant even longer work hours. The unexpected explosion in growth led to his company becoming bloated. And the work continued to mount up, until he could barely take it anymore. During a trip to London, he suffered a breakdown.

It was at this low ebb that Ferriss committed to making a change. Dissatisfied with how he ran his business, he decided to streamline everything. His goal was to delegate as much work as possible to others, freeing up time for him to pursue his true passions.

Out of this revelation came *The 4-Hour Work Week*. And from there Ferriss built a whole new business based on his own ideas. Today he's a renowned online personality who's seen as something of a guru for the overworked.

That's his personal brand at play. Fuelled by the emotional impact of his own story, Ferriss inspires others to cast off the shackles of the 9-to-5 life.

When it comes to branding being fully congruent with integrity, Ferriss is an interesting case. His story of how overwork led to a breakdown is one that many can relate to. It allows him to engage an audience and lends him an authenticity on which he can both build a brand and offer new ways for people to address their own issues of work stress. He understands that your efforts need to work in tandem with the business you're building. If you are to be an influencer people will choose to follow and stay with over the long term, you need to tie your brand to your values, your integrity and your character.

A strong personal brand with integrity — you

In this book I introduce you to the 12 seats at my table. I show how I prioritise each trait, emotion and attribute in order to become a leader people follow. *Integrity before brand* means setting up a strong foundation of integrity and then building your brand. To succeed in business you need both, but you have to get your priorities right.

Whether we realise it or not, every one of us has a personal brand, which we showcase through everything we say and do.

For leaders, entrepreneurs, speakers and influencers, branding is crucial. Without a strong presence and identity, you can't expect any kind of success. Your personal brand, in combination with your unwavering integrity, will help you to attract people to your ideas and your business.

Here's some valuable advice on building your personal brand.

1. Authenticity

One of the main problems with social media is that it allows people to 'fake' their lives. Far too many people use it to show off their lavish lifestyle, or to project a false image of themselves that they want people to see and believe. And that includes many celebrities. Those who don't present themselves in this dishonest way often enjoy much greater success, though. This isn't just about numbers but about engagement. Being relatable helps you connect with others and makes them feel like they truly know you. The easiest way to achieve this is by simply being yourself, rather than concealing the flawed and mundane aspects of your life.

2. Standing out

The purpose of having a personal brand is to give people something to recognise you by. In a wild sea of images, noise and ideas, you need to rise above the crowd and consistently send out original messages. Everyone has something that sets them apart, so it all comes down to finding your particular identity. If you haven't yet done so, the best thing about this is that you can always create something that people haven't seen before. You can find any number of examples in social media, on TV and in the traditional media. It's crucial, however, that you don't simply copy what others are doing, as this undermines the very concept of standing out. The key here is to be bold and to experiment with different possibilities until you find one you think best suits you and what you stand for.

3. Consistency

Once you find the one thing that sets you apart, you need to reinforce it as much as possible.

Your message and values need to be consistent with your brand, and vice versa.

You can have variations but they should still fall within your main brand. This can be a bit tricky as you really need to determine the point beyond which you lose the sense of your brand. Oprah and Ellen DeGeneres, for example, are as consistent as they come. Both built their empires on a simple yet powerful message. Through encouraging positivity and kindness, they found their way into the hearts of millions of people across the globe. They introduce all kinds of innovative ideas, but all of them have a strong connection to the core of their brand. If you fail to send a consistent message, you'll confuse people about who you really are. Being a jack of all trades won't get you far in terms of branding, so make sure to stick with what you do best.

4. Branching out

As contradictory as this may sound after the previous point, you don't want to keep doing the same thing over and over again. There's a difference between being consistent and being boring. Branching out maintains people's interest while still allowing you to send a consistent message. When tapping into a new field, make sure not to lose touch with your main area of expertise.

5. Creating something new

Every brand should offer something of value to the world or at least your immediate industry. It doesn't have to be ground-breaking, but it needs to have some impact on the way others think about or do things. Creativity and innovation are the key to building a personal brand that is unique and powerful.

6. Making connections

Most celebrities are aware that what they do needs to make meaningful connections with people so their brand retains its popularity over time. The same goes for your personal brand. But connecting with your audience is only part of the equation. You need to connect with others to help them spread the word about your brand. More often than not, it's the unlikely connections that have the biggest impact. So if you are looking for a new way to reach more people, try joining forces with other influencers who share similar values and goals to you. Collaborate on various events and projects and you'll see the impact this can have on expanding your brand.

7. *Avoid actions that don't feel like you*

Once they reach a certain point in their career, some celebrities can turn anything into success. This doesn't mean that they should, however. By accepting any deal that will win them more money and fame, they risk having to pay for this by losing touch with their brand. This is why those with a strong sense of their message never do things that are off brand. Taylor Swift, for example, has famously declined many movie roles because they didn't 'feel like her'. As an influencer, you might get a chance to explore topics or promote ideas or products that don't match your personal brand. However appealing or rewarding they might seem, it's best to walk away from these offers if they don't support your message or align with your values.

IN A NUTSHELL

Let's be realistic. Today you have to build your own brand if you're not to be overlooked. It's as simple as that. However, when you start to build your brand, or you revisit your brand at any given moment, ask yourself these critical questions:

- Does my brand fully reflect my own integrity?
- Does my brand show what I stand for and believe in?
- Am I proud of the person reflected in my brand?

The answers you give yourself will help you use your brand in order to stand out and be recognised for the right reasons.

CHAPTER THREE

VISION
before mission

Vision and mission are both of the utmost importance for all of us as leaders, influencers and entrepreneurs. But to clearly define the two concepts, we need to understand the difference between them. Vision, for me, is about focusing on that ultimate dream, that big aspirational goal, the thing you most want to achieve. It's also your legacy piece, what people may say about you in the eulogy at your funeral: *You made a difference in the world in this way...*

In order to put your ultimate vision into words, start by asking yourself questions such as: *Where am I heading? Where am I going each day? What can I possibly achieve in the future? What does my future look like? What do I want to offer the world?* If it's strong enough, your vision will guide you throughout your life.

Your mission describes the things you and your team do every day that align with your vision and will ultimately help you achieve it, or at least come close to doing so. Defining your mission will help you to understand how your values tie into your work, your own goals and your ambitions for others. A mission statement expresses in words the positive differences an individual, company or organisation aims to make. It describes who we are today and how we'll keep working tomorrow.

At our global organisation, Speakers Institute, our vision is to become the leader in speaker training across the globe.

This bold statement declares clearly what we aim to achieve, but we know we're not there yet. Today Speakers Institute is the leader in a number of countries but certainly not across the globe — still, that's where we're heading!

Our mission describes what we do each day. At Speakers Institute, our mission is transforming leaders to become influential speakers. To achieve our vision through this mission is why everyone in our organisation, including our hundreds of volunteers and thousands of clients, have come on board. We all want to see our vision eventually become a reality.

Our vision and mission statements were composed collaboratively by our team. Now, several years on from their formation, we all recognise how these short, sharp, powerful statements give everyone the same road map to follow. We check in with our mission statement in our daily decision making and actions, and we refer to our vision when we have to make big decisions, for instance about the direction of our company.

The world is full of opportunities, as you'll discover when building your business and expanding your role as an influencer. And you'll need to explore each one to determine if it's useful for you. The most powerful way to do this is to look at each opportunity through the lens of your vision. Does this opportunity serve your vision? If it doesn't, then you have to be courageous and give it a pass. If an opportunity or an idea or a potential business partner is misaligned with your vision, then you'll discover that there's power in walking away. It might save you from a disaster, such as a loss of income or a hit to your good reputation.

Create your own personal and professional vision

Everyone can form their own personal vision. The greatest way to define and create your vision is to start by finding people who know you really well and who love and respect you. Talk to them about your thoughts, the ideas going around in your head and what is critically important to you. Then ask them to help you refine and condense those thoughts into one or two essential truths about you. From these you can craft your personal vision statement. Alternatively, work with a coach who will help you to talk about the things that truly fulfil you and are important to you.

The vision for Speakers Institute is broad enough that we can create hundreds of different types of products and remain within the framework of our mission. We can draw on a variety of scenarios in order to deliver our services. When you create your vision, make sure it's broad enough to accommodate any pivot your organisation may take in the future. In March 2020 during the COVID-19 pandemic, like many others we had to restructure our business almost overnight in response to the need for social distancing. We shifted from being an organisation that was all about meeting and teaching people face to face, convening gatherings of hundreds of people, and bringing together our Speakers Tribe for workshops and discussions, to one that does everything online. This raised enormous logistical issues, of course, but it didn't undermine our mission or move us away from our vision. At a time of massive change, we remained true to the three essential guides for our business — our values, our vision and our mission.

So I encourage you to create a vision broad enough that you can pivot to meet any new economic or social challenge and any shifts in the types of products or services you decide to offer.

Ultimately, you want to create a vision that is congruent with your life and values. Only once you have done that can you start to plan your mission.

Communicate your vision

A vision statement should not only be written down. You need to say it out loud, shout it if you like! Talk about it with your colleagues and clients; include it in your pitches and conversations.

When it's spoken aloud, people around you in your organisation hear it and will be accountable to it.

Prior to settling on the final wording of your statements, you need to start communicating the essential ideas and thoughts, even before you decide how best to articulate them. Keep communicating and watch how these ideas are received by others. You'll soon discover what does and doesn't resonate. Sharing these early versions widely and seeing how they land will help you find the words that will ultimately influence others most effectively.

If you want to build a productive, high-performing team, it is very important to constantly communicate your *why* — that is, the vision statement that articulates what you are all aiming for.

That way, everyone will get on board with you and will understand what they need to do each day to move closer to your goals. Everyone will work toward achieving the same agreed ends.

The biggest lesson here is to communicate your vision constantly. The more you communicate it, the more it will resonate with people, because you'll keep getting better at communicating it.

I am determined to make a difference through my own life and work, and for me that means striving to reach our vision. An essential part of this ambition is how I communicate our vision — my dream — to others. A good leader should be able to communicate complex things in easily comprehensible ways.

The greatest failure in communication is to be quickly forgotten. For others to catch the vision, a leader needs to learn how to communicate it so clearly and articulately that when someone hears it, even for the very first time, they can go out and tell others about it.

One thing I believe our team at Speakers Institute have done really well is communicate our vision clearly and succinctly so anyone at all, having heard it once, is eager to share it with their family and friends. Consider one of the most popular TED talks, 'How great leaders inspire action' by Simon Sinek. The underlying message, to 'start with why', couldn't be simpler or more powerful. What's most important isn't *what* you're doing or *how* you're going about it, but *why* you're doing it. My eight-year-old son could understand that.

As communicators, influencers and leaders, we need to learn how to communicate in bite-size chunks that listeners can easily absorb. Then every one of those listeners can become an ambassador for what they've just picked up from you. I believe this is why so many people now tell us they share our Speakers Institute vision.

The vision is so much bigger than me and what I could ever achieve on my own. It's a collective, shared vision; it's *our* vision. And those people who share it with us — our teams around the world, our volunteers and Speakers Tribes, and our clients — are all part of our ever-growing community.

Reach for the stars

I believe your ultimate vision *should* be unachievable. You can go a long way towards reaching it but it should be so big, broad and bold that you'll never really get there. Let's look at our vison statement again: *The leader in speaker training across the globe.* There are around 200 countries in the world, and across the globe there are thousands, if not tens of thousands, of speaker training organisations, many of them very good. So it's going to be very, very difficult — probably impossible — to achieve that goal in my lifetime. But that's not going to stop me from aiming high and striving to make our vision a reality. While we can't attain it today or tomorrow or perhaps even in 100 years' time, we can still set our sights on that destination.

Here's a story I love. Even on his deathbed, drawing in his last breaths, the great Walt Disney was still creating and designing and chasing his vision.

Don't let anything stop you. You might not have the finances or the staff or the followers yet, or ever, but never reduce the scale of your vison. My vision is so much bigger than our resources that I don't know how I'm going to achieve it. I don't know where I'm going to find the resources to do it. But actually achieving a vision is not its only purpose.

One of the main reasons our organisation attracts more than 400 volunteers every year is that they're captivated by the vision and have taken ownership of it. There is power in connecting your own vision with something bigger.

If you are to become a leader worth following, you need to keep open to new possibilities for your future, even if they appear unattainable, and to hold tight to those big, audacious goals, because people follow big visions.

One reason why so many people around the world are turning away from politicians is the feeling that though politicians and bureaucrats might have a well-considered business plan and might even have a mission, they lack a vision. In cases where they do have a vison aligned to their values, they are letting themselves and voters down because they are not communicating it clearly and successfully.

Be bold and brave with your vison. Recognise it's something to strive for even if you never reach it.

And the braver and more creative your vision, the more clearly you can share it, and the more people will want to come on board to help make it happen.

Your mission's there for you every day

Once you have created your vision, the time has come to work on your mission. Remember, vision comes before mission. Your mission is the means by which you step closer, day by day, to realising your vision. It is a statement that stays true to and congruent with your ultimate vision.

Your mission statement gives direction to what you and your team will do each day. So when you come to compose it, work collaboratively with the leadership team, the owners and founders, and the staff to create a short, clear statement. It's a statement that everyone can refer to and rely on, whether they are dealing with clients, making daily decisions, managing the finances or fulfilling any other role.

I see my mission as an inner driving force that gives me focus and discipline, and helps me achieve daily goals while remaining conscious of my own integrity. In practical ways, the Speakers Institute mission helps us manage our company's finances, staff and operations; it also assists us in attracting the best new staff and a wide range of clients.

Your mission keeps you aligned with your vision. On the flipside, if your vision and mission are constantly in misalignment, then it's time to stop and reassess.

Is the strategy behind your mission not the right one? Is your vision no longer congruent with you or your business? Has the world changed so much, as we experienced in 2020, that you're forced to review your goals and your strategy? It might take a global shift to bring you to review your vision, but it could be an ongoing misalignment between your mission and the way you work that makes you reassess aspects of your mission.

Stay true to your mission and then your vision

In 1972, psychologist Walter Mischel, a professor at Stanford University, ran an experiment that came to be known simply as the Stanford marshmallow experiment. This is essentially what happened.

One by one, a succession of children of around five years old were brought into a room by a researcher and offered a simple choice: they could eat the marshmallow on the plate in front of them right away (thereby enjoying instant gratification); or they could wait 15 minutes for the researcher to return with a second marshmallow, doubling their treat (delayed gratification).

In follow-up studies more than 10 years later, Mischel and his team found that the children who had exercised greater self-control by choosing to delay and increase their pleasure went on to perform better academically and to show greater competence in a range of other areas. You can find videos of the initial test on YouTube or read about the study in detail in Mischel, Shoda and Peake (1988), 'The nature of adolescent competencies predicted by preschool delay of gratification,' *Journal of Personality and Social Psychology* 54(4): 687–96.

So why am I sharing this? Because it's a clear example of how patience, self-discipline and determination will win out over grasping the first tempting thing that comes along. If eating two marshmallows is your vision, why settle for eating only one just because you can have it quickly? If you want to achieve big things in your life, to find true fulfilment in your finances, your relationships, and your progress towards realising your vision, then you have to stay on mission in order to achieve that outcome and come closer to realising your vision.

Next in line is the business plan

Your vision statement arches over everything you do in your business. Your mission statement helps you work towards achieving it. At the next level is your business plan, also called a strategic plan. The business plan will change depending on many variables, such as staff numbers, the economic climate, even national and world events. You and your team will review it at least annually to make sure it's still efficient and in sync with current conditions. You might also develop a five-year plan. All the plans and strategies you work with at levels below your mission statement will take into account the shifts in the environment in which you are operating.

IN A NUTSHELL

'Where there is no vision, the people perish: but he that keepeth the law, happy is he.'
Proverbs 29:18, King James Bible

Whether or not you are religious, all leaders and influencers can learn from such wisdom. Define your vision, articulate it clearly and concisely, communicate it broadly, and you will have taken the most important steps towards reaching your goals while staying true to your values.

Values, vision and mission provide the essential foundations for any organisation. Recruit people who are of like mind in these three areas by communicating your vision clearly and strongly.

Our vision statement at Speakers Institute states boldly where we want to head and what the end of the journey might look like. If you want to be a leader and influencer that people will follow, then you need a vision that shows exactly where you are heading and why.

PAULINE NGUYEN ON VISION BEFORE MISSION

Our visions have to be big. They have to be much bigger than ourselves, then we can work backwards from there to achieve them. I believe that if you are to call yourself a visionary, you must see things differently.

A vision is crafted so that everyone can see, feel and imagine it. Our vision, our credo at our restaurant, is to lift the human spirit. Lift the human spirit through the alchemy of flavour, hospitality and heart. I think a vision is so clear that anyone can understand it. Some people might think it's an unusual vision for a restaurant, but I don't mind. If we have an unhappy customer who complains that everything tastes sour or bitter, or if they have an issue on the day, we still try to lift their spirit. Often it works, and we lift our own spirits even higher too.

I have many employees in the restaurant and many students, and I very rarely 'inflict' my mission on them, but I passionately share my vision.

I don't inflict my mission in my restaurant because everyone is at a different level of development. The executives, the managers have their level of development in terms of education and life experience that is very different from that of someone who's just come into the country and is doing part-time work as a dish hand, or someone doing casual work as a waiter who has goals in other areas.

My restaurant, Red Lantern, is what I'm best known for. It's the most highly awarded Vietnamese restaurant in the world. I have my finger in a lot of different pies, but I'm sure that's true of a lot of entrepreneurs. It's not about the bright shiny objects. It's a focus issue. I have a lot of people in my orbit to help me to focus.

I spend most of my time now teaching and speaking about spirituality and entrepreneurship. I write, I travel the world and

I speak. I teach a lot of the contents of my latest book, *The Way of the Spiritual Entrepreneur: The 7 Secrets to Becoming Fearless, Stress Free and Unshakable in Business and in Life*. Spirituality, in my view, has nothing to do with religion; it's about being in spirit and inspired to do our best work. The more in spirit and inspired we are, the better we come to know ourselves.

I have a rule that I only teach and speak from direct experience. People can smell a phoney a mile away. I grew up in very difficult, violent circumstances, and looking back now I know that was my training for following the way of the Spiritual Entrepreneur. My first book was a very dark and personal memoir. It was called *Secrets of the Red Lantern*. It was a very beautiful story about personal freedom and family and hope, which I disguised as a cookbook so people would buy it. It worked, and it became an international bestseller. My second book, *The Way of the Spiritual Entrepreneur*, disguised as a book about a spiritual entrepreneur, is really about alleviating suffering and magnifying human potential. So that's my personal vision and mission for this book.

On whether everyone should have a vision, my first thought is that I don't like to use the word 'should'. It depends again on their level of development. Not everyone wants to achieve. But having said that, those in my orbit, the entrepreneurs in my orbit ... in order to accelerate in life, we absolutely must have a vision.

If you're looking for your purpose, ask yourself what makes your heart sing? Don't answer this by reference to what someone else has said you should do or what you should love. This is about what truly makes your own heart sing. Then ask, what does your life already demonstrate? You can follow a path of discovering a little bit more about yourself and what you want over time. That self-discovery is a beautiful process, and if it changes later on, don't worry about it. Go down that road, and start designing yourself, designing your life. What kind of life do you want?

At first, people might tell you that you are out of your mind when you follow your vision. Stay with it and get out of your mind, because the biggest callings do not show up in your head, they show up in your heart. So get out of your mind. Stay with the vision. Trust it and, as you do, watch how the world forms and moulds around you. Because when you listen to your vision and you live your genius, you become a visionary. Your dogged determination and your unwavering internal certainty will support you. In turn, you will elevate and inspire the people around you.

Everyone is at a different level of spiritual development, a different point in their life experience. So as leader of an organisation and as a personality, how can I inflict my mission on another person? That's not right. My values will be very different from the other person's values. My mission will be different from their mission. But what I can do as a leader is to passionately share my vision. And if everyone can feel that vision and see that vision, they can work towards it. Use all your skills to paint a picture of your vision that everyone can see, so those in your circle can share the vision.

Pauline Nguyen is one of Australia's most successful entrepreneurs — but with a difference. She combines a high-performing Western business background with an Eastern spiritual sensibility.

Pauline approaches everything she does with an unshakable spirit, and this has carried her to prosperity. While running her much-awarded restaurant, Red Lantern, she has written two bestselling books, *Secrets of the Red Lantern* and *The Way of the Spiritual Entrepreneur*. She holds a BA in Communications from the University of Technology, Sydney, and in 2008 won Newcomer Writer of the Year at the Australian Book Industry Awards. In 2012, Pauline and Red Lantern won the Australian Telstra Business Award for Medium Business.

CHAPTER FOUR

CONSCIOUS
before decision

You might say that the definition of a good leader is someone who can make quick, well-considered decisions. Think of a firefighter or a nurse or even a sports captain. They don't have time to stop and assess all the pros and cons. Their decision making is based on their training and experience, and they must often draw on their own inner strength to help them make the right decision. They don't act on their emotions but find a calm point in their mind where they can think clearly, conscious of the many possible implications of their choices.

> **If you want to be an influencer people will follow, confident decision making is essential.**

When you have to make a decision, are you conscious of:
- the needs of the stakeholders
- the way the decision could affect the people around you
- how the decision and its outcome fit into the vision of your organisation
- the implications of *not* making the decision?

Some people find it easy to make decisions. Others find it harder, and some often find it almost impossible and tend to procrastinate until it's too late. Yet no matter how we feel about it, we all have to make thousands of decisions every day in our personal and professional lives. As an influencer whose time is in demand from every direction, you will need to find ways to make good decisions quickly and with clarity.

As an influencer, you're in the spotlight, and people will judge you and your actions to see if you are a person worth following. This can add extra stress to the decision-making process. Make the wrong decision and your reputation could suffer; make the right decision and others will look to you for advice.

When you find yourself in this position, it is tempting to make a quick decision based on your first response and your emotions, but that won't always lead to the best outcome.

A good leader thinks quickly but makes decisions thoughtfully and calmly, having weighed up the many issues involved and determined the best way forward. An outstanding leader and influencer will also draw on a fundamental tool to help them make sound decisions: I call this their consciousness.

When I make any big decisions, I explore all the ramifications through the lens of my consciousness. This means I'm conscious of how my decision will affect the people involved; I'm conscious of my own beliefs and aims, and whether my decision will be congruent with them; I'm conscious of my own values, and of our vision and mission if the decision affects the business; and I'm conscious of the potential impact, good or bad, of the decision on my position as an influencer.

As my business grew and I began to speak on the international stage, I came to understand that the major decisions I made could have huge ramifications not only for me but perhaps for tens or hundreds of people around me. The weight of this responsibility could have been overwhelming, if it were not for consciousness. I won't always make the right decisions, but I nonetheless feel confident that I have the right decision-making process in place.

The five-stage process

This is my own decision-making process, which has consciousness as its foundation.

Stage 1

Tap into your intuition and listen to what your gut and your heart are saying. Always follow your instinct as it will usually guide you to the right path. Let's explore this more deeply.

Your own personal intuition, your gut feeling, is a powerful tool that you ignore at your peril.

I've known times when my instinct has told me to go one way while the people around me have told me to go another, and when I've ignored my instinct I have regretted it. Alternatively, when I have seen many benefits in making a certain decision but for some reason my gut feeling compelled me to walk away, I have been incredibly grateful.

With some of the decisions we make, especially in business, it can take a long time and, sometimes, a lot of money before we can conclude if we made the right call. What might seem like a great idea at the time can turn out not so well in the future. So trust your instinct and follow your heart—after all, they're an important part of who you are. Having said that, don't let your emotions control you. I believe your instinct and your emotions are quite different. By following Stage 2, you will protect yourself from letting your emotions alone influence your decision making.

Stage 2

Rapidly process the consequences of making the decision one way or the other. Think of it as a quick SWOT analysis (Strengths, Weaknesses, Opportunities, Threats) to help you make the right decision. This is where you complement your initial gut feel with objective analysis. Collect all the information you can to fully assess the various potential outcomes of the decision. This process can take time, if it is available. If you have to make a major decision quickly, follow the same process but aim to speed it up. Give yourself a few moments to clear your head, make a quick objective assessment based on all the information you have at hand, then decide.

Stage 3

If the time frame and situation permit, find one person you respect with knowledge in your field who can offer advice and with whom you can bounce around ideas. This might be your partner or one of your staff; it could be a manager or a leader within your team. If you have more time, gather opinions and advice from a range of experts — a mentor or coach, and perhaps members of your board or your leadership team.

It's essential that you really trust the people you turn to at this time, and equally important that they understand your situation, including the context in which you're making the decision, and are conscious of the fundamental factors involved.

When assembling your decision-making team — which could be your board or advisory committee — look for individuals who have:

- walked the same pathway you are setting out on
- known you for a long time, so they are loyal to you
- the same vested interest as you, so you can trust them.

Stage 4

You will now have a high-level advisory group or board with whom you can discuss important decisions. Next, assemble a second-tier group from the team you work with every day. This group might include a marketing person, a PR person, a finance manager, a creative director and an HR manager. These people work closely with you in your organisation. They are conscious of the needs of the company, its staff and clients through daily experience and understand its vision.

There are now three tiers of contributors to the decision-making process: (1) you, (2) your senior-level advisory board and (3) the people who work with you in running the company.

Stage 5

This stage might surprise you, but I have found it both an important and a reassuring part of my decision-making process. Without it, I know I would have made some seriously bad decisions that failed to align with my values. It's where you go when you're making some of the really big decisions in your work or personal life; where you can draw on a level of self-enlightenment, if you like; where you transcend the everyday to gain a bigger picture of the impact a decision could have. Some people may turn to their god for advice, some to meditation; some may take time out on their own for quiet contemplation in which to give the process their full attention. By now you will be fully conscious of the range of elements you need to consider. It's time to tune in to the deeper part of your consciousness and your sense of personal integrity.

Decision makers

As I've said, some people find it hard to make major decisions and need to be encouraged to draw on their confidence to back themselves. Then they can stand with courage and make their own decisions. Others have so many voices around them, so many advisers, fans or critics, that they end up passing on the ultimate decision making to someone else. They've lost their consciousness, and along with it their sense of integrity and their courage. Why? Because they've allowed other people to make decisions for them.

If you find yourself in a place like this, where you are frozen and unable to take responsibility for your own decision making, it may be time to step away from those advisers and work on your own strengths in order to find yourself again. To build your self-confidence, look at what you have achieved already.

Collaborating is great but to be an influencer people will confidently follow, you also need to know your own mind.

Being fully conscious of your situation and the consequences of your decisions will help you to form your own opinions with clarity.

Your mindset

Your mindset influences the way you make decisions. If you have a fixed mindset you are more likely to take a cautious approach; you might even try to avoid putting yourself in a position where you're expected to make major decisions and instead try to delegate that responsibly to others. You'd prefer not to change the status quo.

By contrast, people with an open mindset will often see the decision-making process as an opportunity to learn and grow. An entrepreneur starting out may be prepared to make a risky decision with unpredictable consequences as it could lead to something amazing. They understand it could fail, but they see making a wrong decision as part of their development. They know they can learn and grow from such experience, perhaps not straight away but eventually.

Personally, I really don't have a lot of regrets. If I make a decision that turns out badly, I stand back and look at it through the lens of my consciousness. I try to understand what when wrong, what I could have done differently, and I use the experience as an opportunity to continue to learn and grow and develop my own wisdom.

Building your confidence to make the big decisions

If you think fear, anxiety or a lack of confidence are stopping you from making decisions, it could be useful to examine these feelings and how they might be holding you back, then flip them in order to achieve a positive outcome. If you still find it difficult to make decisions or you're afraid of making the wrong choice, give some thought to the following considerations.

Look to the future with excitement

Don't dwell on the past. What happened then does not have to happen again now or in the future. Adopt an open mindset, and think about the opportunities that could be waiting for you in the future. In a meeting with one of our speaking clients, we identified that the main reason she was not seeing the results she had anticipated was that she had not dealt with her insecurities in relation to her past failures. By identifying old patterns that haven't served you well, you can disrupt them and create new ones and move past limiting beliefs.

Be confident in yourself

You can waste a huge amount of energy worrying about what others think of you, particularly when you make the wrong decision. This is when you can draw on the consciousness of the process — look at what you have achieved and what you are capable of doing, and respect your own abilities. This will help you to focus on making the best decision rather than on what others think about you.

Too often we miss out on opportunities because we are so worried about what people think of us. To overcome this, decide on a powerful goal that you are determined to achieve. This will help you move away from needing approval from others. Each milestone you achieve along the way to reaching that goal can be a cause to celebrate and congratulate yourself, thereby building your confidence.

Use positive language

This is perhaps one of the easiest steps to take. Change your way of thinking by changing your language. Instead of 'never' say 'one day'; instead of 'can't' say 'let's have a go.'

Just do it, and don't procrastinate

There is a clear difference between hesitating when making a decision because you want time to gather all the facts, and procrastinating and hoping the decision will eventually go away. Leaders don't have the luxury of procrastinating. They have to decide and act on issues, crises and opportunities as they arise. It doesn't mean you should rush in uninformed, but you can't hold back and hope it will all go away.

Focus on the things you can control

There are things in life that we simply can't control. When something goes wrong that was beyond your control, review what happened and move on. Don't blame yourself or feel defeated. Instead, put your energy into the things you *can* control.

Stay in the positive moment

We all make mistakes. Some people learn from the experience and move on; others can't seem to leave it behind. It consumes them, growing bigger and bigger in their mind, yet they are unable to learn from it and walk away. A measure of an inspirational leader is that they take responsibility when something goes wrong, then they *bounce forward*.

Embrace change

Change is happening more rapidly today than at any time in history. Being flexible and having the agility and resilience to navigate change successfully is what leaders do daily. Decision making and change go hand in hand; if you want to be someone people will follow, embrace them with confidence.

IN A NUTSHELL

We all make thousands of decisions every day; in both our personal and our business lives we face decisions with potentially huge outcomes. At this level, you need to start the decision-making process by being conscious of your values, your goals and the ways you want to demonstrate your significance. Once we are conscious of all the implications of a decision, we can examine the practicalities and arrive at a considered choice.

If you want to lead and influence, you must have the courage and the clarity to make good decisions. Often this will mean making them on the spot, when you don't have time for research or to stop and think for too long. When that happens, you should be ready to draw on your conscious awareness of who and what is involved in or affected by the decision. This will help give you the confidence to act quickly and with authority.

CHAPTER FIVE

COMPLETENESS
before purpose

First of all, let's explore the nature of purpose, because the word *purpose* is used in many different contexts: 'What is the purpose of your company?', 'What's the purpose of your actions?', 'What is your purpose?' I associate purpose with moving forward unerringly towards achieving your chosen goal. When you have a true purpose, nothing will lead you off the track that's taking you where you need to go. When you're clear about what you want and where you're heading, you can identify your purpose and define your personal mission, or that of your company or organisation.

However, in order to be clear in your own mind so you can focus on your purpose, I have found that you first need to feel complete within yourself. By this I mean that any negative issues in your life you haven't dealt with—such as anxiety or stress, anger or frustration, even boredom—anything that makes you feel like you can't be bothered, will hamper your ability to work out exactly what your purpose is.

You first need to feel a sense of completeness, because only then can you start to explore where you are headed and set out for that place of purpose in your professional or personal life.

So how do you feel complete? In my own experience, that sense of completeness comes from a place of deep gratitude.

Gratitude

Gratitude is fundamental to what I do every day, what I believe in and how I interact with others. An attitude of gratitude is an intrinsic starting point when I'm reaching for a positive outcome. It's where I must begin if I'm to find and maintain the strength and energy to continue.

Each one of us has different aims and a different purpose, but we all need to focus on our pathways to see where we are going in order to reach our own unique goals.

There are so many reasons why we lose focus on our true purpose. We may feel that someone has offended us. It's nearly impossible to be grateful and offended at the same time, so deal with why you feel offended. Talk about it with the other person, work it out, come to a resolution if you can, then put it aside. Do everything you can to replace the feeling of being wronged with one of gratitude. If you are finding it hard to achieve a sense of completeness, first explore all the reasons in your life why you should feel a sense of gratitude.

I live with a disability. Every single day since that car accident in October 2006 when I lost my arm, I have felt physical pain. When I close my eyes I can still feel each finger on my right hand, my wrist and my elbow, as if they were still there. Sometimes the phantom pain in my right arm is so strong it wakes me up in the middle of the night.

I could live with an ongoing sense of frustration or anxiety or stress, or even depression, knowing I only have one arm. And that my other arm is now just a stump that causes me constant pain. But instead of yielding to those negative emotions, I enjoy a fundamental feeling of completeness. Why? Because I have discovered deep gratitude. I survived a life-threatening accident; I have lost an arm and can't bend my right leg, but I am still mobile. I have one good arm and I'm grateful for it. I have one good leg and I'm grateful for that too.

This sense of completeness has given me the clarity through which I've been able to find my place of purpose.

Australian author and thought leader Nick Vujicic was born with no arms and no legs, yet if you look at his photo on the cover of his bestselling book, *Life Without Limits*, you'll see his big, generous smile. Having met Nick, I can vouch for the deep courage and strength that keep him going. He knows he is complete within himself, which lets him focus with clarity on where he wants to head with his purpose. He's an internationally acclaimed speaker and founder and director of the organisation Life Without Limbs. Nick knows he is complete, and he knows his purpose.

If you spend a lot of time thinking about what's wrong in your life, you're not going to find your clarity. Your thoughts will be clouded by everything you believe has gone wrong. But if you come from a place of gratitude, even though you're not perfect and like all of us you have your flaws and hurdles to overcome, you can find your own completeness. And once you're complete within yourself, you can turn your focus towards where you're going in your life, your purpose.

It was only after my accident that I found my true sense of completeness. I felt like I was looking through the eyes of someone totally different from the person I was before. I now look at my family differently, and I see my purpose and my destiny in a different way. Let me explain through a personal example. When he was 19 years old, my younger brother, David, was diagnosed with leukaemia. He went through radiotherapy and chemo, but those treatments didn't work. As a last resort I donated bone marrow to him, but sadly that didn't work either. David passed away when he was 21 years old. In our family we all recognise that by the time he died David had made a unique contribution; his life was complete and he'd fulfilled his purpose on the planet.

I'm still alive even though that car accident could easily have killed me, and every day this brings me a sense of completeness. As I see it, I survived for a reason and a purpose. I now go through life motivated by this thought: *I've been given a second chance. I've actually been given a second life.* Maybe before my accident I took much in life for granted. I don't do so now.

I recognise different levels of gratitude. The number one level is gratitude for the simple things in life — for the air I breathe, the clothes on my back, the money in my wallet, the food in my fridge, the roof over my head. Most of all, for the family I love and who love me. And the simple fact of still being alive — for me that's where my gratitude starts and it's the source of my completeness. I know I am alive today for a reason and a purpose.

My gratitude for the good things in life means never being complacent.

I believe that I am so focused on achieving my goals in life because of the simplicity of my gratitude. I'm achieving great results in my life because the birthplace of my focus and purpose is the deep gratitude I feel that I'm alive today. I could have died, but instead I lived. But it's more than that, because my sense of gratitude was with me as a child and supported me in dark times as a teenager, even if I wasn't fully aware of it then.

My gratitude is reignited when I visit developing countries where I meet people who appear to be so much less fortunate than me. If you're feeling hard done by and less than grateful for your lot in life, try visiting a community where people don't enjoy the privileges, comforts and physical safety you take for granted. It just might create an *aha* moment that brings you to ask yourself, *Well, what do I have to complain about?*

Finding your sense of completeness

Here are some tips to help you find your own completeness.

Start by asking yourself how you are feeling

What is bothering me today? What is worrying me? What is pulling my focus away from my purpose? Once you have identified those worries, look for ways to address and overcome them. Some problems might be too big to handle on your own. You should never be afraid to ask for professional help. Other problems might be dealt with simply by talking about them with the people around you. If someone has done something that leaves you feeling upset or incomplete, talk to them about it. If one of your colleagues appears to be working against the best interests of your company or organisation, ask them why they are doing that, and try to help them towards your vision of the business.

As a leader, you need to step up and ask the difficult questions to help everyone find a resolution and move forward.

Assess your state of mind

How do you feel about yourself, the people around you, your job, your career? Do you enjoy a positive frame of mind or do you feel something is missing in your life, making you feel incomplete? If that's the case, try to work out what you can do to change it. Again, be open to asking for help, whether from friends, colleagues or professionals. Your state of mind can change from day to day, so take the time to assess your feelings each day. If you go into a meeting feeling less than complete because you are worried or angry or upset, you might not be able to see your purpose clearly and objectively. As a leader and a team member, don't let others down because your state of mind is letting you down. Be prepared to do something about it if you can, and find your completeness.

Look honestly at your story

If your mind is filled with limiting beliefs about yourself, or you're sharing a story about yourself that will make others think you're not good enough, or confident and strong enough, then you'll be incomplete. Change your story and get rid of those limiting beliefs. If you need help for this, ask for it. People usually want to help, especially the people around you who share your purpose.

Look at what you do each day

Your personal sense of completeness can be tied in with what you do each day and how you do it. Be ready to try something new or do something in a different way. Be open to changing elements of your life so you can feel more fulfilled and be in a clearer place to define your own purpose.

Use your strengths to become complete

Many different assessment tools are available to help you find out what your core strengths are. I've found the Gallup StrengthsFinder really helpful. You could also use Myers-Briggs, DISC, or a number of other personality profiling assessments.

Work with a mentor

To harness your strengths, I recommend you work with a mentor. Find the right person who can help you to identify the source of your greatest sense of achievement; this way you can find your own completeness. Your mentor can also help you define and discover your purpose. I don't believe you can find your purpose by yourself. You need the right people around you to help you to draw it out. I talk often in this book about the importance of having a mentor because no one should feel they are alone.

Some people resist turning to a mentor or coach out of pride or arrogance. Their attitude is *I can do it myself* or *I don't need anyone else telling me what to do*. Others feel too shy or resist admitting they are vulnerable and need help. To all of these people I would say, bury your ego, or raise up your self-confidence and find someone you trust who will listen to you and help you realise your full potential.

When you're looking for a mentor, reach out to someone who has been there and done that, who has earned your respect through what they have achieved in your area of interest. I once came across someone who was offering advice about how to write a bestselling book. I found I didn't agree with the advice offered, so I asked him, 'How many bestselling books have you written?' And the answer was, 'None.'

There are plenty of people out there who would like to mentor or coach you, and even more who are more than ready to give you advice. Everyone wants to offer you feedback, and many of them want to be paid for it, but sometimes that feedback will be wrong or not useful, and it's often hard to backtrack after acting on unsound advice. So choose your mentor or coach wisely. The best way to do this is to ask for recommendations from people you trust in your industry or professional circle.

You need to work with someone who has actually achieved something that you want to learn, who has been there and done that. Just because they have the right 'formula' or the gift of the gab doesn't necessarily mean they have valuable first-hand experience or know how to put the theory into practice.

I am very cautious about who I choose as my personal mentors. I will always ask them if they have personal experience of what they are talking about. Have they been through the highs, the lows, the successes and failures? Do they speak from a place of conviction and knowledge rather than just confidence? Are they prepared to really listen to me and consider the best advice they can offer *me*, even if it isn't always the easiest advice to take on board? I want a mentor who will tell me the truth, lead by example and be genuinely keen to help me achieve my goals. This is the type of mentor you need too.

Completeness as a leader

A leader worth following will make sure they are complete in themselves before they engage with a situation, conversation or decision that is critical to their organisation. They'll make a major decision only when they know they have dealt with anything that is distracting them or making them feel incomplete.

The best leaders recognise that when making decisions, 'It's not about me, it's about we.'

They lead with a real sense of 'I'm already grateful. I'm good. I'm okay. You guys don't need to help or mentor me, I'm going to help you. I'm going to serve you. I'm going to be there and be present for you.'

A leader who has checked in on their own sense of completeness can inspire a sense of purpose in other people. And as I've noted, often the first step in feeling complete is to feel gratitude. Acknowledge what you have, what you have achieved, the strength you draw from people around you, and you will be in a positive frame of mind for tackling the problems and issues facing your business or organisation. Once you have checked in on your sense of completeness, then you can strive to achieve your purpose.

Completeness is appealing

When a leader lives with a deep and sincere sense of gratitude and completeness you can see it in their face. There's a lightness about them; a genuine warmth and love and sense of empathy shines from them. They have the confidence to treat people with respect and even compassion where appropriate. They won't be looking at ways to big note themselves — they don't need to. Instead, they will be looking for ways they can best lead, support and serve others.

A leader is most effective when they have dealt with their 'inner demons' and negative emotions. They deal with them by developing their sense of gratitude.

This doesn't mean they won't ever get angry or anxious or depressed. These are natural emotions and part of what makes us human. How can you show empathy if you haven't experienced lows as well as highs in your life? But you need to know how these feelings and experiences influence the way you lead, the decisions you make, the way you deal with people. Draw on your sense of gratitude and completeness to help you through the times when work or life is hard for you and for those around you.

Acknowledge any demons that might be holding you back as a leader and influencer. For all of us, there are things in our life we're not overly proud of. It could be a bad habit or a little bit of backstabbing or gossiping, or something you do to your body, such as drug abuse, smoking or excessive drinking. Once you have recognised and acknowledged your demons, work to drive them out or you will never feel complete or achieve your purpose. If necessary, ask for help, talk to health professionals, put in place a plan you will follow to push those addictions or bad habits out of your life. But also be kind to yourself and remember that it might take time, it probably won't be easy, and even the greatest leader or influencer sometimes needs to ask for help.

When you find your own sense of completeness and you are aligned with your purpose, that positive feeling will stimulate you, motivate you, and make you a stronger, more appealing and compelling person to follow.

Now focus on your purpose

Once you have reached your place of completeness, you can then focus on developing a deep sense of purpose. It will give you the strength and commitment to stand up for what you believe in. I like to say that once aligned with your purpose, you will be ready to stand for something rather than fall for anything. Once you clearly stand for something, you will inevitably draw the trolls, but if you don't have trolls chasing you, then you're probably not making a big enough difference in the world. With a feeling of completeness and a commitment to your purpose, you are prepared for any criticism, because you're no longer craving acceptance or trying to please everyone. Now it's about being true to your purpose, and your purpose is your daily mission; it's with you all the time.

Let's look at the impact this can have on your standing as a leader, an influencer and a speaker.

People don't really want to listen to someone who claims to be able to talk about anything. They may have plenty to say, but they're unlikely to have anything of real value to offer if they haven't dedicated themselves to an area of expertise or a particular industry.

People like to see that you have a true sense of purpose, and understand what it is and how it can be achieved. They want to hear a clear message, and you need to show them why they should care about it and want to share it. Anyone can tell a story. It takes a real influencer to tie their story into an overarching message and purpose that persuades others they should care.

Susan Tardanico is a speaker and the author of *Beating the Imposter Syndrome*. She points to purpose as being extremely important. In an article for *Forbes*, she writes, 'Before you start working on your script or presentation, get clear on its purpose. What are you trying to accomplish? What impact do you want to have on your audience? Are you looking to inform? Inspire? Persuade?'

Once you know your purpose, you can identify your audience, your market and the people you want as your colleagues.

With a defined purpose in place, you can say, 'This is what my purpose is and this is who my message appeals to.' From there, you can highlight your credentials and continue building your authority as an expert in your field. You can build your standing as a thought leader, and people will come to you because they want to share your purpose.

IN A NUTSHELL

Outstanding leaders, managers, influencers and speakers know their purpose and are committed to achieving it. As the first step in this journey you should become complete within yourself. Do this by working out what might be bothering you. Are you anxious, angry or stressed? Do you feel someone has let you down, or worse? If so, then find ways to deal with these issues. Ask for help, talk to the people around you, address the problems and, importantly, find your sense of gratitude. Look at what's great in your life; think about the people who give you their love and support; consider the good things you can do for others and how you can change even a small part of someone's life for the better. That will bring you to a place of gratitude and completeness.

Once you've reached this place you can make clear decisions, unclouded by negative emotions or bad habits. Bring this clarity to achieving your purpose and you will be someone people want to listen to, and your sphere of influence will grow. You will have a positive impact on the people at your table and beyond.

CHAPTER SIX

TRUST
before influence

Most people want to exert an influence on others. We want to influence our friends, our family, our community. We want to influence others in our workplace and, certainly, our marketplace. We want to influence our team and our clients. We are growing more and more sceptical, though. We feel we've seen it all before... we've seen how corporations and governments try to influence us but all too often abuse our trust. Our leaders and managers, businesses and brands are all trying to promise us things and sell us things. Our growing scepticism means the future of influence has to be based first and foremost on trust.

Trust

As a leader, what value do you put on trust? What value do you put on trust if you are a follower, a colleague or a client? How important is it for you to know that the leaders in your life are ethical and prepared to speak out for the good of their community and to speak out to protect the truth? Do you show through your actions that you have integrity and you are someone people can trust over the long term?

Answering these questions will help you to determine the kind of leader and influencer you can be.

As a professional speaker in the influencing space, I often heard from booking agents and other speakers that after the global financial crisis in 2008 one of the most in-demand topics in personal development was ethics. That was particularly the case in the finance industry in New York. Experts in the field of ethics were asked to go in and literally teach financiers about morals, integrity, core values, ethics and truth.

More than 10 years later, we are still looking, with mixed success, for leaders who value truth and whom we can trust, be they politicians, business owners, teachers or mentors. Among the generation of young people entering the workforce today, many are looking to start careers that offer some benefit to the world and are looking for charismatic leaders with a strong ethical foundation and character. And they are asking this question even before they ask what they will be paid — that's how important it is to them. This generation often puts character before money.

These young people recognise that it will be a scary world in the future if we don't bring truth, transparency, integrity and character to the forefront of our work and private lives.

There is a widely held perception around the world today that our politicians are not trustworthy; that they are more concerned with appealing to the greatest number of people rather than showing character and speaking the truth. I'm not saying this really is the case, but if this is the way politicians are seen, then the time has come for them to show through their actions that they can be trusted and are committed to truth telling. They need to show what they stand for, to demonstrate their authenticity and integrity. Voters want to know what their leaders are prepared to work hard to achieve for the good of the community; they are sceptical about those who just come up with a smart sound bite or an over-friendly handshake for the media.

We all need to lead in our own way, in line with our principles. If you think politicians or other influencers are letting people down, then it's up to you to draw on the strength of your character and lead in a way that is trustworthy and positive.

When you have earned someone's trust, they will lend you their ear. On the other hand, when someone starts preaching to you or telling you only the things they think you want to hear when they're selling you a product or service, your scepticism kicks in and you stop listening.

Trust has to be at the core of our communication before we can influence others.

Trust comes from authenticity and also from vulnerability. We no longer want to hear from our leaders and influencers that they have everything under control when clearly a situation needs serious attention. We don't want to hear people say they've always been successful and never faced setbacks. What we're leaning into now is listening to those people who admit honestly that they have sometimes fallen short, those people who say, 'Hey, look, I've failed many times, but I've learned how to overcome that failure. Let me share my experiences and what I've learned with you.'

Vulnerability and authenticity are the building blocks of trust. If you create trust through your own authentic, vulnerable, transparent story, you will win the ear of your audience. That's when you can become an influencer people will respect.

One of the best ways to win someone's trust is by speaking from your heart, being as transparent as possible, being truthful about your pain and your failures as well as your successes. The more vulnerable and open you are, the more people will be ready to lean in and listen to what you have to say.

One of the concerns of the decade

Trust, or a trust deficit, is something that people around the world are really concerned about at the start of this new decade. This is particularly evident in our perception of big companies and the marketplace. As consumers we are growing ever more aware of what we are buying and we're asking lots of questions before we take out our credit cards. We're now demanding that manufacturers and retailers be transparent about their supply chains — about where their products are sourced, their impact on the environment and so forth. And we expect to be told the truth. We're saying, 'Hey, be transparent and show me who you guys really are.'

The integrity of businesses, leaders and influencers is always under scrutiny. It's something the public and the media check on regularly. For example, an influencer on social media might have thousands of followers, but they can do one thing wrong, or perceived to be wrong, and their followers will turn against them in a nanosecond.

You can do a whole lot of great things for the planet and for humanity, but one perceived bad move and you can quickly lose all the goodwill you have built up with your consumers. It's as if we are forever searching for flaws in other people's characters, signs that they are untrustworthy, because that's almost what we've come to expect, and sadly there's little room for forgiveness nowadays. One sign of untrustworthiness and it's going to take hundreds of positive touchpoints to win back the trust you once enjoyed.

People on every continent crave leaders and influencers they can trust. Show me someone who's building a movement or a tribe, who's leading and standing out as an influencer in the most positive way, and I'll show you someone who embodies trust and transparency. Because trust comes before influence.

A LEADER COMMITTED TO THE TRUTH

Mahatma Mohandas Gandhi stands out in history as a heroic figure, both in India and around the world. His dedication to peaceful protest played a huge role in India's struggle for independence. He was both a moral and political leader of his country, known by many as the Father of the Nation, an exceptional influencer and a man deeply committed to the truth.

Born in 1869 in Gujarat in northwest India, Gandhi trained as a lawyer in London, returned to India for two years before moving to South Africa, where his experiences of racial injustice drove him to campaign for civil rights. It was through his political activism in these years that he developed his philosophy of nonviolent resistance. Returning to India in 1915, he soon threw himself into the independence struggle. Over the many years that followed, his tireless work inspired an entire nation to believe that decolonisation and self-government were attainable.

By 1942 political tensions in India had reached an all-time high. The seeds of rebellion against British rule had long been planted. On August 8 they sprouted into a full-blown movement when Gandhi delivered his famous 'Quit India' speech in which he called for an immediate end to British rule and launched a campaign of nonviolent resistance to achieve that goal.

The next day Gandhi, along with most other leaders of the Indian Congress Party, was arrested and imprisoned by the British authorities. His speech inspired the nation, united the Indian people against British rule and created the nonviolent protest movement that would ultimately lead to Indian independence.

Gandhi's moral stature and leadership by example changed the course of history. His call for peaceful protest was an extension of the life he had always led. He lived by his values, which lent his words total authenticity. He left

(Continued)

no room for misinterpretation of his beliefs; for instance, he was always careful to target the institutions of British colonial rule and insist that the people themselves were not the enemy.

Gandhi's ambition was simple: human rights and freedom for all Indians. He struggled to contain the threat of sectarian conflict between India's two dominant religious communities. Independence, he insisted, should not spark a war for power between Hindus and Muslims. He called for unity, mutual respect and tolerance. Gandhi brought together those with conflicting beliefs and ideologies in a common cause, and in doing so he reinforced his commitment to tolerance and cooperation.

It would be another five years before India finally gained independence. Gandhi was assassinated just a few months later, triggering a terrible bloodletting as many of Mahatma's hopes of unity were dashed. Nonetheless, today Gandhi is universally recognised as an inspirational figure of peace. The Indian people were prepared to follow him despite the heavy costs because he exemplified selflessness, truthfulness and authenticity, making him a leader people could believe in.

Vulnerability is a sign of truthfulness

Most of us prefer to hear the truth in someone's story, even if it's hard to cope with, than to be told lies that suggest the speaker has known nothing but great success. We value truth and authenticity, and that is what we look for in our leaders.

We admire sportspeople for their athletic exploits. Great athletes can inspire others to do amazing things. After all, they push the boundaries of physical achievement and show us what's possible with our own bodies. In this way, a great athlete can be an influencer.

In 1939, an American sports hero, Lou Gehrig, stood on a baseball field and delivered one of the most moving speeches of the 20th century. His complete honesty won him a place in history that matched his sporting achievements.

Born in New York in 1903, Lou Gehrig was the son of German immigrants. He grew up in abject poverty. None of his three siblings survived infancy and his father was an alcoholic. However, his mother was a hard worker who constantly pushed her son to educate himself, and it was at school that Gehrig began to show a talent for physical activities. In particular, he had a gift for baseball that none of his peers could match.

Gehrig graduated from high school and won a place at Columbia University, where he starred in both the football and baseball teams. His batting ability drew the attention of the New York Yankees, who signed him up in 1923. Thus began the professional career of a baseball legend. Gehrig went on to play 2130 consecutive games for the Yankees. Along the way, he won many championships and enjoyed a career that made him a shoo-in for the Hall of Fame.

Suddenly, during the 1938 season, his performances began to suffer. Disturbed by his drop in form, Gehrig checked himself into the Mayo Clinic for testing, which was when he discovered that he had amyotrophic lateral sclerosis (ALS), a condition that forced him into immediate retirement. In front of the fans that had cheered him on for over a decade, Gehrig delivered a powerful retirement speech that offers so much for influencers and thought leaders.

Gehrig's speech was loaded with vulnerability. It was clear that the ALS diagnosis had devastated him. It was also clear how much he would miss the sport he had loved so much his entire life, yet he showed no self-pity and remained positive throughout the speech. Though he faced a life-threatening challenge that had taken away so much that he loved, he was not going to allow it to grind him down. His bittersweet closing line showcases this courage perfectly: 'So I close in saying that I might have been given a bad break, but I've got an awful lot to live for.'

With these simple words, Gehrig confronted his own vulnerability. He put it out in the open for all to see before declaring that his diagnosis would not prevent him from enjoying his life. That's one of the reasons why his audience connected with him during his speech. Many had grown to idolise him for his playing abilities. But in showcasing his vulnerability, Gehrig gave the audience a reason to care about him as more than just a very talented ball-player.

IN A NUTSHELL

Many of us want to influence others. Around the world people are looking to thought leaders for new ideas and directions. But at the start of the new decade, we are growing impatient with people who want to lead and influence on their own terms. Instead, we're looking for leaders who will tell the truth, for better or for worse; who will bring us into the conversation by sharing with us what they believe is going on.

We are ready to listen to people who admit their vulnerability by sharing their failures as much as their successes. And we are ready to throw our support behind inspirational leaders, like Gandhi, who commit their entire lives to fighting for what is right and true. In this decade we will be influenced, perhaps most of all, by people who stand up for the truth.

TONY TAN ON
TRUST BEFORE INFLUENCE

Trust means everything to me as a business owner and leader. If there's no trust, people will not take action — that's what I believe. And if they do take action without a basis of trust, it's just half measures. You have to be totally committed to your message and what you have to offer before you can consider taking it upon yourself to make changes and become an influencer.

In my own life, wanting to influence people began with the realisation that the world needs clarity. But even with that understanding, I wasn't ready. It was not until I took up speaking and got more involved in it that I realised I needed to give myself a voice and help others gain clarity.

Looking back on my career, to be honest, I never planned to be a business owner. It was the 1997 dot-com crisis that changed things for me. I was given an opportunity to set up my own company; I had the right people around me and I had the business model.

In life and business, there will always be times of crisis when you need to know you can put your full trust in the people who're working through those problems with you. If you don't trust each other, how are you going to solve the issues and get through the crisis? Without trust, how are you going to build a business together?

It's always important to show customers they can trust you. And your staff too. You want them to follow you every step of the way. You need to earn their loyalty. If they don't trust you, they won't trust your policies, they won't trust that you're right. You won't get 100 per cent performance from your staff if trust isn't established first.

Trust is a journey, not a destination. Throughout this journey you will earn the trust of others by your actions, and you'll be tested along the way. Sometimes it might seem easier to go off track; when you feel that way, use trust as a guiding principle to bring yourself back.

The notion that 'you must earn my trust' is absolutely right. You cannot just give your trust away. This world is made up of a lot of different people, and some are manipulative and smart at playing their own games. They might seem trustworthy, but when you put your trust in the wrong person, things can turn bad very quickly. So it's important that you slowly build up your trust in someone. Trustworthiness is something that must be proven.

I'm currently developing some technology to teach people how to influence others through AI (artificial intelligence). I hope to empower as many people as possible and give them a voice to go out there and use their influence positively. Of course, there will always be a segment of the community who will use technology in ways that might not be congruent with what I want to achieve. But I've learned that a person can only be incongruent for so long. Sooner or later their true character will show, and these people will get filtered out over time. Their actions won't stop me from developing a platform to give people the voice they need, because I believe in the common good.

By 'character' I mean the way people are committed to doing good. My view of goodness means helping and serving society in a positive way.

Thinking about the future, I want people to be empowered, I want people to embrace AI. That's why I build technology platforms — so people can see how AI can impact them positively, and how technologies are there to help them to progress in their lives.

I want to build myself up as a speaker and get clarity around AI. Having the right tech is one thing, but making sure that people embrace it, reducing their anxiety about its adoption is another. At this time I'm looking at both an inner world and an outer world. The outer world is technology. The inner world is our mindset, the mind space. Are people ready to embrace AI? Are people ready to look at it positively so they're able to transform their own lives? I want to bridge the outer and inner worlds, helping as many people as possible towards the right mindset, the clarity and the practical understanding to embrace technology to enhance their lives.

One of the most important ways to build people's trust in me is through giving them factual data and evidence. Instead of just telling them, I show them the evidence to influence them towards making a decision. References, case studies, research and personal example all come together to create a multifaceted approach to show how this particular technology works.

In this context, my personal example is absolutely critical. You cannot talk about something as an expert if you haven't done it yourself or if you're not a living, breathing example of what you are preaching or teaching. If you don't have the credibility, you don't have the trust. People could ask, 'Why should I even listen to you? I mean, who are you? You can tell me anything you want, but that doesn't mean I will take action based on what you've said.' I want to show that I'm a successful example of someone who is embracing this technology. By showing them that you've been there, done that, others can say, 'Yes, this guy is the real deal. I can trust him. Now he has influenced me.' That's why I agree that trust comes before influence.

Tony Tan is the co-founder and deputy CEO of Imperium Solutions, an AI company that has received more than 20 industry and business awards. He is also a global speaker, an author and a business leader focused on 'the future of disruptions for AI'. Tony has helped more than 300 000 corporate users — from Fortune 500 companies to government agencies — optimise their business results by leveraging the power of AI. He is also the creator of the AI2 framework, which fuses the potential of AI with the strengths of humanity to give birth to 'the AI Powered Influencer', a new-generation influencer who communicates powerfully and creates stronger connections with optimised productivity.

CHAPTER SEVEN

VALUES
before action

The actions we take — from how we show up each day to how we exercise, how we look after our health, our wellbeing, our spiritual life — are all based on conscious decision making. And our decision making is tied to our values, or it should be. Acting without reference to our values can be ill-advised.

When I was young, I didn't recognise the importance of basing my actions on a strong foundation of values. In high school I wanted to feel worthy, to feel good enough. I wanted to be liked. I was quite unconscious of my values and how they could and should serve me. The way things played out, I thought I'd found my worth when I started to be liked by the naughty kids. They were the classroom disruptors, the ones who tried drugs and alcohol, the kids who were not academic, who were in fact quite destructive. Though they were a toxic force in my life, I craved their approval. I began acting irresponsibly. A part of me knew I shouldn't be acting this way, but at that time my values weren't strong enough to stop me.

I got kicked out of school. Which came as a massive surprise to me.

I asked myself, *Are my values serving me well now?* I had to really re-evaluate what exactly was the foundation I wanted to build my life on. What was my value system? This questioning process helped me to realise that I had to 'stand for something or fall for anything'. This idea has stayed with me, and even today it helps me say no to ill-advised actions even when under pressure to say yes.

Going through the process of identifying and defining my values as a young man helped me to build the foundations of the value system on which I've based my life ever since. That value system still helps me take the right actions in the right situations to find fulfilment and success in my life. I didn't go through this process on my own. Kate, who became my wife, was there with me.

I had to experience that crisis moment in my teenage years to find my value system. I'm certainly not suggesting that we all need a crisis moment. The best way to find your values, however, is to take advantage of a high-pressure situation to decide what you are willing to compromise on and what you are prepared to act on. To decide, in other words, what you stand for.

Your value system is pivotal to the actions you take every single day.

If you're concerned that some of your actions could be detrimental to you or others, take a look at them through the lens of your value system and let that be your guide.

As I found, the process of working out your values isn't easy, so reach out to people around you for support. I had Kate. You might have family, colleagues, mentors or a coach.

Sharing your values

I believe the greatest way to share your values with your team, or even with your family, is to adopt Simon Sinek's formula: First ask, 'Why?' and only when you've clearly answered that question can you ask, 'How?' and 'What?' For more on this, read Sinek's book *Start with Why*.

When we were setting up Speakers Institute, everyone in our small team was given a seat at the table. Together we discussed what the company's core values should be. We wanted to move away from a top-down structure in which the owner or CEO tells the staff what the company stands for. Instead, everyone was encouraged to contribute and be a part of the process of determining and articulating our values. There are many reasons why this process was productive and successful; one was that creating our value system together ensured greater buy-in from every member of the team.

Here are the five core values that we all agreed on as the foundational principles for Speakers Institute.

TRUTH
We are a team that are true to our word and operate with absolute integrity.

BELIEF
We are a team that believe unequivocally in everything we do and everyone we work for.

PASSION
We are a team that is passionate and enthusiastic about learning and delivery.

COMMITMENT
We are a team that is committed to producing extraordinary results.

EXCELLENCE
We are a team that strive towards excellence for all our clients.

We are committed to these values and they influence every action we take as an organisation.

When we sat down at the table to discuss what our values should be, we talked about how many key values our business should focus on. Eventually we agreed that five were right for us. They covered the work we do — our actions — as well as our motivation and goals. We encapsulated each value in a single sentence — a declaration, a short, sharp statement that is memorable and easily understood, and is at the same time 'macro', covering a lot of ground.

These five values are the fundamental building blocks for the actions we take every day of our working lives. They are displayed conspicuously on our office walls all around the world and on our website. We rely on them daily, referring to them in conversations with colleagues and clients, so they gain a deep insight into what we stand for.

When new staff members join us, we share with them the story of why and how we created these values collectively; what each of the values means to the company as a whole and to every individual in it; and how they guide us in our everyday practice — in our actions, our business conversations and our decision making. We also discuss what each value means to us personally — that is, our *why*. In this way, we aim to ensure that everyone working in our company respects and adheres to the five core values.

The culture within our work community ensures we keep each other accountable for our value system. If someone is compromising our agreed values, then no matter what position you hold, you are free to pull them up, and say, 'Hey, is what we're doing right now congruent with our values? Does this align with who we are?'

By setting our values collaboratively, we had created a culture through which we can keep each other congruent and accountable, and aligned with these values.

The core values are a foundational element of any culture, the DNA of any team that works together.

If someone on the team isn't aligned with the company culture, it can be massively toxic to everything and everyone. So if they're not willing to change and embrace our values, then they have no place on our team.

Values and actions speak to us

Clients and customers are drawn to organisations and businesses by both their values and their actions. A company may make a big call and do something really bold, causing us to wonder, *Why are they doing that?* When we peel back the layers to find out what's happening we discover, *This was actually in alignment with their values, so that's why they've made that call!*

The company might be acting very differently from usual but working fully within its value system, and this can be very exciting. It's a good sign for staff and clients and anyone else looking on, as it shows a company that is operating on firm foundations but is willing to take new directions. That can capture people's attention and make it an attractive organisation.

Organisations don't necessarily advertise their value systems in the marketplace, whereas they do advertise their actions. Increasingly, consumers are smart enough to see past those actions and look for the values behind them.

At the level of the individual, an influencer and leader worth following is someone whose foundation of values informs their everyday actions.

Taking bold, brave actions that align with your values will make you an attractive leader and influencer.

Many corporations have lost our trust in recent times. Why? Because they've taken actions that are based not on values but on monetary gain or the desire to make it to the top at any price. An organisation that enjoys longevity, or a true leader worth following, will be prepared to forgo financial gain or status if the actions needed to achieve these things are misaligned with their values.

The point I want to make here is that there's a difference between acting completely in line with our core values and meeting only our basic obligations. Companies might deliver services that tick all the boxes from a compliance point of view — they might meet all their contractual obligations and follow the law — without going a single step further. A company worth dealing with, an individual worth following, will go further and deeper. They will aim to offer the very best service or product in a way that is most congruent with their core values.

Courage

It takes courage to make big, bold moves as a leader, an influencer or an organisation. Even more for whistleblowers who are brave enough to stand up and publicly challenge corruption or dishonesty in their workplace. Think of companies that refuse to use products in their supply chain because they are produced by child labour. And consider those individuals who will speak up for what they believe in even if it means being trolled on social media, or worse. These are examples in which core values and courage together lead actions.

Again, if you don't stand for something, you'll fall for anything. A reason why some organisations struggle is that they fail to hold to their value system. It takes bravery, and often sacrifice, for a leader to take a stand against all the odds. There's no courage in taking actions that compromise your values, but taking action that aligns with your values even though it pits you against all the odds — that is true courage.

Your support team

At the start of the chapter I described how, as a young man, I came to understand that I needed to define my values, and how I was supported in this endeavour by my future wife, Kate. The experience taught me the importance of finding the right mentors to guide me — people I deeply respect.

The people I most respect are those who have themselves taken a stand when the odds were stacked against them. In a mentor I look for someone who isn't a people pleaser, who walks their talk, whose every action is congruent with their values; who's not out for a quick buck or just to have lots of people like them; someone who is willing to stand up for what they believe in, no matter what. That's the kind of person I respect. Someone you respect who has walked in your shoes, so has a personal knowledge of your experiences, will understand what you are going through or aiming for.

Your support can often come from your colleagues. I keep my team accountable for our values, and I urge them to call me out on these values too. In our leadership team meetings, for instance, as the business owner I might be looking to save a bit of money, so I'll say, 'Hey look, let's do this ...' But if someone in my team says, 'Sam, I'm not sure this is a good fit with our values,' it would be remiss of me to not stop and consider if this criticism is valid. The pressure I feel as CEO sometimes puts me in a place where our value system isn't front of mind, which is one reason why we need to declare our values loud and clear, why I encourage others to return to them whenever we are making important decisions and why I am not in the least offended when others rightly call me out.

The bottom line is this: we all wander away from our values at times, so as a leader you need to create a culture in which your people will feel safe to pull you up — in a constructive and respectful way — when you stray. To be an influencer people will follow, you need to be held accountable. If you're not, your pride and ego will take over and you'll think, *I can do it all myself—I don't need to listen to anyone else.*

I have an advisory board, and there are times when my advisers annoy or frustrate me, or even make me angry, but they teach me too. As a leader, I need to grow constantly, and I'm not going to do that unless I have people in my life to coach and mentor me and keep me accountable.

The further you are along on your career path, and the bigger the team you're leading, the easier it is to forget your values.

I've mentioned how, as a professional speaker, every time I walk off the stage, I find a line-up of people waiting to sing my praises, to take a photo with me, to get my autograph. After 15 years of this, it's hard not to get a big head and an inflated ego. I see this happen with many influencers.

When I recognised that this was happening to me, I realised I needed to shield myself from temptation. This might sound strange, but being a speaker on the international stage attracts admiration. This is a great compliment, but let it get out of control and you can quickly lose touch with your values. When the people you love and respect ask, 'What about the values?', that's the moment you need to stop and realign your actions to what you believe in.

Values and actions align

Every seat at the table is filled by an element that is essential to help you become a leader or influencer people will want to follow. But that doesn't mean there aren't other elements that are important. These might apply at the level of what you do day to day. We need values to lead and inform us and actions to put those values into practice.

Let me share an example of how our five values at Speakers Institute can align with our actions.

A major firm approached us to work with them on a project. We had been recommenced because other clients had found that we have integrity and that we deliver 100 per cent on what we agree to — our value of Truth.

They wanted to meet with us, so two of my colleagues went along. As everyone in our team respects our five core values, I knew that the two going to that meeting would represent us well. This aligns with the value of Belief.

Our value of Passion is one we enjoy. We share a passion to deliver the best service. My colleagues went to that meeting fully prepared, with ideas to share; they arrived on time to ensure they didn't waste people's time. They were looking forward to finding out more about the project and thinking of ways we could contribute to it.

Commitment is a value that informs the energy we put into our work. At the meeting, my colleagues showed through their actions how they would listen to the client and work with them to deliver a program that would best meet their needs.

The client respected our actions and saw us as a professional, trustworthy organisation, an organisation that would deliver Excellence.

We secured the contract.

Your clients might not know what your values are but they will judge you by your actions, and the two are closely connected. We look at it this way: *Values before actions, and actions that reflect values.*

Your value proposition

A value proposition establishes what you can offer your clients that sets you apart from others. It is commonly used business terminology, along with KPIs and USP, but it's something else too. I think of our value proposition as our formal commitment to making a difference by serving our clients, contributing to our community, and giving true value to our clients and even to other staff members. When your value proposition is to serve the people you lead and the business you run, you have set the groundwork for acting in a way that aligns with the values of the organisation and the staff.

Create your value proposition with your team so everyone buys into it and contributes to it.

Work on it at two levels: the level of action, where the value proposition helps guide what you do; and at the more fundamental level, where the proposition promotes your values, and brings others in your proximity on board to come up with ideas that could lead to a better future for your team, your organisation, your community.

IN A NUTSHELL

Our days are filled with making decisions and taking action — in our workplace, at home and as we plan for the future. Action is essential, of course, but what happens when your actions lead you to the wrong place in your life, as happened to me as a teenager? What if you're confronted with a major decision and you're not sure which way to go? What guides you as a leader and influencer that people want to follow? The answer is your values. Values come before actions, because your values inform your actions, helping you to navigate the countless major decisions we all have to make through life.

CHAPTER EIGHT

LOYALTY
before opportunity

When starting my business, I seized every opportunity that came my way. Why wouldn't I? After all, that's one of the best ways to build a business. And I encourage you to do the same. I'm always open to considering new opportunities and I'll always take the time to evaluate if a new approach may be better than the old way of doing things, or if a new service will bring more to our organisation. For all entrepreneurs, grabbing the right opportunities with both hands is the way forward.

At the same time, I'd urge you to look back over your shoulder to check that you aren't leaving anyone behind. Are you remaining loyal to the people who supported and taught you? Equally, are you leaving your fundamental dreams and goals behind without realising it as you chase each new opportunity?

Loyalty

Loyalty reaches out in many directions. There's loyalty to a mentor, a coach, to your parents, your friends, your partner, a person in your upline.

There's also your loyalty to your dreams and your goals, ensuring that you stay focused and don't change course, that you stay in your lane. You need to hold on firmly to your loyalty to what you believe in and value and never lose sight of it.

Thirdly, you may be loyal to a group or tribe that you're part of and is important to you, perhaps a local or virtual community, an association, a church or other organisation. These people are important to you in so many ways. Don't be afraid to demonstrate your loyalty to that group; if it serves you well, then ask yourself why you'd want to move on to the next new thing.

Staying loyal in the hard times

As a leader, you will be known by your character and your loyalty. When crises arise and life gets hard, a deep sense of loyalty to the people around you can keep you going and give you the opportunity to show your unwavering support for them too. Loyalty will give you the grit that's needed to make it through the low times.

The strength of your loyalty to a person, an idea or an organisation will be remembered when the storms pass and the good times return.

You will be respected for loyalty that stays strong no matter what is happening around you.

Loyalty means you don't give up easily. You'll keep pushing through, no matter what the frustrations.

Work out if a project or a person or a group deserves your loyalty (it's okay to reassess this as times change). If you decide they do, then give it fully, unceasingly, with a strength and commitment that is unwavering. In your personal relationships, for instance, if you are committed to someone your loyalty to them will help you push through any disagreements or misunderstandings. All relationships have their seasons. It's not all going to be happiness and laughter and fun. You'll have your highs and lows, but loyalty helps you negotiate the lows so you stay together to enjoy the highs.

Some people will give up the moment a storm blows in. Why? Because they haven't built the right foundations and they are not relying on their values and loyalty to help them weather the storm. For me, then, loyalty must have a seat at the table to help each of us build the right foundations, so when the storms do come we don't just jump ship. We stay the course.

It's easy to be loyal in the good times; you won't have any trouble staying loyal to someone when they are popular. A true leader will stay by a person's side when others walk away. When something goes wrong, people talk—they gossip and criticise. There's a ripple effect as more and more people join in the negative conversation. They join in not necessarily because they want to criticise the victim, but because they want to be accepted as part of the group, even if its only common purpose is mud-slinging. I've seen it happen all too often. Proximity to these critics can be toxic. In situations like this, loyalty will help you distance yourself from these people. By this action, you'll be helping yourself, just as you are supporting the person being criticised. If someone earns your support, then give it to them 100 per cent, and don't stand back.

Leadership and loyalty

The traits of a good leader include grit, determination and drive. It's about surrounding yourself with the right types of people, about standing for something rather than falling for anything, about not blowing with the wind just to gain acceptance. Loyalty and commitment are traits we should all develop in our own lives. For a leader, they will help you to set your priorities and protect your values. If you are loyal to a person or a group, you will put their interests first.

Loyalty to yourself

We all look to those around us for affirmation; we're attracted to people who tell us we're doing a good job, reassure us that we're popular. We enjoy connecting with those who tell us what we want to hear. That's only natural. It can be more difficult, though, when we're given tough but constructive feedback. It's not easy, but accepting criticism is important. Some of us welcome it as a challenge and a learning opportunity. For others it's an excuse to walk away, to decide they want to look for new opportunities, to change the circle around them. They'll desert that coach or mentor in the hope of finding others who'll tell them what they want to hear.

We owe it to ourselves and to them to stay loyal to the people who offer respectful criticism and advice as well as compliments.

There's another aspect to loyalty to ourselves that's also important to consider. I have met so many people who have jumped from coach to coach, from one personal development program to another. They chase every new opportunity, join every new group, forever finding new mentors. They're constantly chasing whatever is new rather than backing themselves and being loyal to what they have achieved and to their own expertise. They won't back themselves because all their confidence comes from listening to other people rather than from trusting the person in the mirror.

I encourage you to show loyalty to yourself and what you believe in, to stay in your lane. Commit yourself to your goals, dreams, aspirations and vision. Don't chase every bright new opportunity without asking yourself why? Why do you want it? What do you hope it will bring you? Is it what you need in your life or your business right now? Why do you want to move out of your lane?

After answering these questions honestly, you might still decide to chase that opportunity and it might lead to great things. That's fabulous. Perhaps, though, your answers will show you're really only looking for new opportunities because you're scared of where you are now; you're lacking in confidence, unsure of your purpose. If that's the case, then now is the time to remain true to yourself and your goals, review the way you are working towards them and build your faith in yourself. That bright, shiny opportunity can wait.

I understand through my own experience that when you're starting out on a new career or setting up something new, you need to be open to opportunities. But when you find your lane, stay in it and focus on achieving your long-held goals. This focus can lead you to a place of mastery in your field, along with ongoing success, confidence and satisfaction.

Loyalty to your expertise

Stay loyal to what you know and do well. When you reach that place of mastery, remaining loyal to your core vision, your dreams, you can become a leader and expert in your field. Be loyal to your specific niche, and the opportunities will come.

When I coined the term *Bounce Forward*, it could have been just another fluffy idea that came and went. I could have done a couple of Instagram quotes, written a couple of blogs, maybe even produced some content around it, then moved on to the next shiny thing in search of new opportunities. Instead, I stayed loyal to the idea captured by those two words. I wrote a book developing the concept, then a second. My third book became an international bestseller.

I focused on that idea and I drilled down rather than opening out. Instead of looking for the next shiny thing, I focused. I created content about Bounce Forward for teams, Bounce Forward for organisations, Bounce Forward for finance, Bounce Forward for youth, for teachers, lawyers, accountants. I ran one-day Bounce Forward workshops, delivered keynotes on it and offered coaching. I introduced a six-month Bounce Forward program. I remained loyal to the concept I had created and built a business around it. I became the world authority on the idea and how to put it into action in life. If you do a Google search on 'Bounce Forward' you'll see that I fill the first 14 pages.

It's all about staying in your lane and staying committed and loyal to the decisions you make, even through the tough times.

Gradually, though, time passes and the right moment may come along to move on to the next thing. In my case, I have reached such a level of expertise and ownership of the 'Bounce Forward' concept that it will always be a significant part of what I do. But the time has come to move it aside a little and explore new opportunities. I remain loyal to my vision and know it's broad enough to let me try something new.

When I arrange the 12 seats at my table, one concept doesn't have to exclude others. Loyalty runs deep; it's a commitment you make to others, and they to you. But new opportunities keep businesses going into the future and make life interesting.

The 4 C's

There are four character traits that, for me, are intrinsically linked to loyalty. They are courage, confidence, certainty and conviction.

You need courage to overcome the three human fears: fear of not being loved, of not being good enough and of not being accepted.

Courage means showing up even when a voice inside you says you can't, you're not good enough, you're not worthy, not loved. When you show up, confidence comes along. A lot of the time we tell people, 'Just be confident' or 'Show more confidence'. I don't believe we can turn around and simply be more confident. Confidence is a product of courage. When someone is courageous, confidence shows up. Yet even when you're courageous and confident, it doesn't necessarily mean you're certain.

Certainty, I believe, comes from conviction. Certainty comes from having such a deep conviction in something that you'll stay true to it.

How does all this tie in with loyalty?

Courage, confidence, certainty and conviction are your support team: they help you stay loyal to your vision, purpose and aspirations.

They back you up in times when others try to bring you down. All too often you'll need courage, confidence, certainty and conviction to stay loyal to someone when other people turn against them or simply walk away.

Remember that when you start to make a difference, when you start to implement, to lead other people, the trolls will come.

That's when you'll need the courage to hold true to what you believe in. Because, again, if you don't stand for something, you'll fall for anything.

IN A NUTSHELL

Opportunities are great. They can open doors for start-ups and revive failing businesses. The thrill of chasing a new opportunity is exciting and I love it. But before opportunity comes loyalty.

We should stay loyal to people who have been there for us, even in times when others are rejecting them. We should stay loyal to our goals, vision and purpose, and to our own expertise.

People look to leaders and influencers who have the foresight and creativity to recognise the benefits of new opportunities. More than that, though, we respect leaders who value loyalty and don't lose sight of it in the tempting glow of the next shiny new opportunity.

CHAPTER NINE

SIGNIFICANCE
before success

What do you think of when you hear the word 'success'? Our society so often makes us relate success to a fatter wallet, a nicer car and a home in the right suburb. For some people, success can indeed be linked to these material goods — to having the money to buy the brightest and newest. Beyond what you can buy and own, success can mean achieving your goals, winning your race, topping the class, raising a happy family, and doing your best in your field and your life.

Success is good. It's important for each of us to aim for and eventually achieve success in our own terms. But I believe this can happen only when our values and actions are aligned with our purpose — what we do or intend to do, what we accomplish. When our purpose makes a difference to our own life and the lives of others, it becomes significant.

Success has a broad reach. You can make lots of money, have many followers, achieve great things for your company. There's no denying that these are things many of us quite rightly aim for. But success can also be measured by the positive impact we have on others.

What is significance?

The essence of significance is adding positive value to people's lives. You can focus primarily on personal success and having everything you want, but you can also turn outwards to others and focus on serving and giving value. You can explore ways you might contribute and make a difference in the world, or at least your corner of it. That's when your actions take on true significance.

I realised that my true fulfilment comes from living a life of significance, adding value for others. That's one of the reasons I work in the field of personal development: I can add value to the lives of our clients and audiences. In our company we make a point of discussing and reviewing our significance, and how our actions and purpose align with it. From this position of true alignment, our success has grown. Today we value both our commercial success as influencers and our significance as thought leaders. Our experience has shown us that the more we are aligned with our significance — our meaning as a company — the greater our success.

Significance and leadership

Good leaders know people want to be confident of a leader's intentions before they decide to follow them. Before we get on board with a leader — in business, politics, organisations or universities, for instance — we first need to question them on their intentions.

How do they define success? More importantly, how are they leading a life of significance? Is their intention to make and sell more products, to see their company's share price rise, to beat their competitors and be the best and most successful financially? That's all great. These people are good business leaders and help keep the economy afloat. We need successful leaders to build and manage companies, organisations and cities.

More importantly, though, we need leaders who are committed to making a lasting difference by contributing positively to society and to humanity. We need to ask our leaders if their purpose and intention are ultimately to serve and add value. Do they want to make an ongoing beneficial change? Do they want to contribute something of real significance to their community and the world?

If you want to be a leader and an influencer worth following, think about the significance of your actions. What is the unique quality that shines through in your values, your actions and your vision that makes you significant as a leader?

When you align your aims and purpose to achieve significance, success will follow.

As a leader, you will get buy-in from the people around you and your team. They will recognise that you want to be successful but, even more, that you want to do something of real significance.

Some years ago, one of the big banks recognised that staff morale, productivity and performance were all dropping. From a number of surveys and data sources, they found that their staff lacked a sense of purpose and any feeling that they were making a difference. So the bank's management decided to give every staff member one paid day a month when they could volunteer for a local charity or for their chosen not-for-profit organisation (the choice to be approved by management). They encouraged and supported everyone's participation. A few months into the volunteering program and the bank's employees said they had found more purpose in their role. This, in turn, raised their productivity and performance. Why? Because the bank was encouraging them to do something that was bigger than themselves and bigger than what a financial institution usually offered. They were actually contributing and making a difference to their community through their volunteer work. The bank helped its staff to find another level of significance in their professional life.

ONE OF THE WORLD'S MOST SIGNIFICANT LEADERS

Nelson Mandela inspired millions during his crusade to end the apartheid system of racial segregation and black oppression in South Africa. Eventually he changed the future of his country. Mandela led a life of deep significance.

Born to the Madiba clan in the Eastern Cape of South Africa in 1918, Nelson Mandela became one of the most inspiring figures of modern times. He grew up listening to stories about the brave achievements of his ancestors. And these stories inspired him to spearhead the fight for freedom for his people.

In the 1940s, he became politically active and was involved in forming the African National Congress Youth League (ANCYL). In the 1950s, he was a partner in the first black law firm in South Africa. It was during this time that his activities started to come to the attention of the government and security services. In 1956 he was arrested on charges of treason. Though he won an acquittal in 1961, it was clear that his dedication to the struggle for freedom would soon land him in further trouble.

By this time, he and other resistance leaders had recognised that nonviolent resistance to the apartheid government would not bring about change. After helping to launch the ANC's armed wing, Umkhonto we Sizwe (Spear of the Nation), in early 1962 Mandela left South Africa under an assumed identity. On his return towards the end of the year he was immediately arrested and charged with having left South Africa without a permit.

A year later, he faced further charges relating to his work with Umkhonto we Sizwe. Along with nine others, Mandela answered charges of sabotage during the infamous Rivonia Trial.

Everything that Mandela had worked for to this point had the aim of achieving liberation and equality for black South Africans. Now, facing a possible death penalty, he rose in the dock and declared that he would die if he had to in order to achieve a free and democratic South Africa. The trial, and in particular his powerful speech in the courtroom that day, marked a turning point in the struggle against apartheid.

Despite spending the next 30 years in prison, Mandela remained the leader and figurehead of the anti-apartheid cause. Just four years after his 1990 release, he became the first democratically elected President of South Africa.

His strength, courage and unrelenting commitment to crushing the apartheid system made Nelson Mandela a leader who was admired around the globe, and the significance of his actions lives on today.

Success is great. We often celebrate successful people, look up to them and follow them. But success can crash overnight. True significance lasts after we've left our leadership role, and can even survive our death. If we have made a positive impact on people's lives, we will always be significant to them.

On 5 December 2013, Nelson Mandela died at the age of 93. Years on, the memory of the 'Father of the Nation', often called by his Xhosa clan name, Madiba, is still respected, not only in South Africa but internationally. His significance in world history will never die.

We follow leaders who put significance before success

These days, many of us, including young people who are joining the workforce for the first time, are driven more by our purpose than by the attraction of a big pay cheque. We're motivated by a desire to make a difference in the world, a social consciousness, a greater purpose, a meaningful destiny.

Leaders need to share with their team what is significant for them. They should also share and discuss the vision and mission of the organisation or the group they lead.

As a leader, you should always be conscious of your impact on your staff, your team and the people around you, and how you might inspire, inform and even transform them.

This can be done through your words and actions — that is, by the example you set — and through the strategic direction of the company. It can be done by talking about what is critically important for you in your life and asking others what is significant for them, and what significance *means* to them.

As a manager you have to keep a close eye on the company's incomings and outgoings. You're always analysing spreadsheets. 'Okay, we're making this much money,' or 'We're losing money — we have to change our strategy.' These are the conversations you have with your colleagues, perhaps daily, as you work to make your business a success. An inspiring leader will take this a step further by discussing how the activities of the business and everyone working in it will help to achieve something of significance. A good leader in the workplace will aim for both — financial success and significant actions that will inspire teams to make a lasting positive difference.

A leader worth following will communicate the significance of making a difference and giving value, which will often flow through to commercial success.

IN A NUTSHELL

Success is exciting, fulfilling and often lucrative. More important, though, is the significant contribution we can make to our community, our organisation and the people we lead. Success can be fleeting; it can rise and fall within a year. True significance is lasting; it is a legacy you create for those who follow. It can make all the hard work, overcoming obstacles and knock-backs, worthwhile.

I wish you all success for the significant achievements you plan for your life.

FADZI WHANDE
ON SIGNIFICANCE
BEFORE SUCCESS

Significance before success resonates with me because I don't know anyone who has become successful without having put themselves out there in the service of others. To be truly significant, you need to make an impact on others. Being in the business of wanting to transform, inspire and have a positive impact requires empathy. You need to think, *What can I do?* or, *How can I use my skills to benefit other people?* Tapping into that empathy is how you become significant.

My own journey towards making a difference to other people's lives started early. I didn't have the best of childhoods. If I think about what I went through, one of the things that was significant for me was that I really didn't have anyone to talk to at that time. So, through my own experiences, I developed an affinity for people who would otherwise be forgotten. In school I was drawn to the kids who were singled out, and I think my feelings of empathy started then. I'm still constantly looking for groups or individuals who are on the fringes of mainstream society and thinking about how I might help them.

I also have a deep faith, and many of the things I do are inspired by my beliefs and my desire to live a life worthy of this faith. I realised that if I truly want to create any form of legacy, I have to think about how I can leave the world better than I found it. I know it sounds clichéd, but that is truly how I live my life.

After going through a really bad divorce I was feeling lost. I didn't know who I was and I was trying to find myself. So I started volunteering for a lot of different organisations, and that's how I came to be involved with the Australian National Committee for UN Women. This gave me the opportunity to go to the Commission on the Status of Women, which is held every year at UN headquarters. I was part of the five-member delegation from Australia. That was the start of my process of changing my life.

Before that, for so many years I had been seeking validation in my life. I did an MBA because I thought it would mean people would see me differently, but it didn't change anything. There was still an emptiness inside. It was only when I started tapping into the things that I was passionate about, that aligned with my values, that I felt a change. When I think about inclusion and diversity, for me it really is about my life experience, the countries I've lived in, the times I've felt like I wasn't valued or respected. I pour that understanding into my work.

I truly subscribe to the idea of significance before success because I've seen it in my own life. My success, however you want to define it, such as in terms of building a big profile, has come as a result of the fact that I wanted to make a significant contribution to the lives of the people around me.

Success for me is when I go into a room, engage with somebody there and by the time I leave they have the confidence to make a change in their life. Through our conversation they have learned something; it has had a positive impact on them — they want to be better. Also, when I decide I want to be better at something in my life and I take action, that to me is success.

Everything I do is about legacy. It's about what people will say and think when I'm not in the room. If people tell me that I've made a significant contribution to their lives by sharing my story, that to me is success. That's what I want to be remembered for. I want others to be able to say that I loved people and that I fought for the rights of the underprivileged. I want people to say that I was godly, I was God fearing, and that I was somebody who was dependable, who was committed, and who raised my sons in a way that they are now men who have also earned respect by fighting for justice for others. That's really what I would like people to say about me, that I really cared deeply and my whole desire was to live a life worthy of the gospel. I always ask myself, *Is my life reflecting the faith that I hold dear?*

There's a saying that I came across some time ago — I'm not sure who wrote it: 'You cannot strengthen the weak by weakening the strong.' It serves as a reminder of the fact that, to be strong, to be significant, it isn't about setting myself above others or taking advantage of people who might not have the influence I have. I want to make life better for others, especially those who are on the margins. If I can do that, I will be a success, but more important, my life will have significance.

Fadzi Whande is a global diversity and inclusion strategist and social justice advocate. Her work focuses primarily on addressing systemic and institutional barriers faced by historically underrepresented groups. She has worked across the not-for-profit, government and business sectors in Africa, Australia, the UK and the USA.

Fadzi has received both local and international recognition for her efforts to champion inclusion and diversity. She won the 2019 Social Impact Award from the Organisation of African Communities, was a finalist for Western Australian of the Year, an Australia Day Ambassador and a recipient of the International Racial Equity Leadership Award in the USA. She sits on the Board of the Museum of Freedom and Tolerance Western Australia, is Deputy Chair of Volunteering WA and is an Ambassador for 100 Women (WA).

Fadzi is an alumna of the Duke of Edinburgh Commonwealth Senior Leadership Program, HIVE Global Leadership Program and Leadership WA Signature Program. She received an Executive MBA and Graduate Certificate in Social Impact from the University of Western Australia.

CHAPTER TEN

SMALL
before big

So often we want the big things and we want them now. We want a big, happy life, a big career, a big salary, big travel opportunities. We want a big profile and big follower numbers on social media. And we want to command big stages and access big areas of influence.

Then when we've decided which big things we want, we aren't content to wait — we want them now. We're not willing to put in the time and effort to go on that long, steady journey towards achieving each big thing — we're in a rush. That's why a lot of people give up too soon, particularly when they're starting up their business. They have big aspirations, big dreams, but they aren't prepared to stick it out and work through the hard times. We see a massive failure rate in start-ups because the people leading these new companies don't realise how tough the journey will be, and how long it can take before you can reach out and touch those big goals.

One of my favourite sayings to live by is: *Be faithful with the small and the big will come.*

Do the small things well, give them your full attention, and recognise that often the small things will grow into something big, something with a major impact on your life or business.

All too often we overlook the small, mundane tasks, or we don't feel motivated to complete them. We may think they're a waste of time or won't lead to anything much. Yet attending to the details, giving every task your full attention and commitment, is imperative as you progress on your journey to achieving success. For example, as an influencer, you'll know that content is king. The more content you produce and release, the more firmly you will be positioned as an authority in the marketplace. Creating your content, such as writing blogs and books, producing high-quality videos, staging events, giving away free advice or incentives, or being active and generous on social media will all contribute to building your profile, but it takes time.

If you want your influence to grow, you need to post valuable content on social media *every day*, but don't then waste time by browsing randomly through what others are saying and posting.

Attend to the small things and your influence will grow big

You use social media in your daily life, but are you making full use of it for your business? Here are some tips for using your content and social media platform to build your profile:

- Close enough is not always good enough. Take time and care when crafting your content.

- Before you jump onto social media to see what everyone else is doing, think about your own posts: what do you want to say, what images or videos do you want to share? Write and prepare the content, attend to the details, then post.

+ Take the time to be social on social media.

+ Reply respectfully and generously to the comments people write on your posts, and comment on their posts.

+ Before you film your next video, take the time to write your script. Draft and redraft it until it's entertaining, informative and engaging.

+ For every blog post you write, do your research, and really consider the content you want to share. Again, draft and redraft. This is how to gain a good reputation and draw people back to your blog to read more.

+ Post often to build up the followers you need as an influencer.

+ Come up with your own unique hook or angle, one that is authentic to you. Doing something unique or different is a great way to gain people's attention. If your hook goes viral, all the better. That's free publicity for your brand.

Bethenny Frankel, American reality television personality, entrepreneur and author, believes strongly in the importance of social networking, but she insists you have to be creative and disruptive — that's right, 'disruptive'. You need to catch people's attention in creative ways in order to stand out from others. Don't be just another blip in their notifications — make people want to read what you have to say.

When you're faithful to the little things, you'll find that big things will come. Before you know it, more people will be sharing and commenting on your posts, more people will be talking about you, inviting you to take part in events and speaking engagements, asking for your opinion and advice. More opportunities will come along, and slowly and surely your standing as an influencer and leader will grow. Instead of influencing dozens and hundreds, you'll be reaching out to thousands and tens of thousands.

From a small staff a big team will grow

Invest in the small group around you if you want to grow big. If you start out with one or two employees, treat them with respect and work with them to develop their own career path. That's one way to build loyalty early on and create a spirit that will support you and your staff as your company grows.

All entrepreneurs feel some degree of uncertainty when they start a new business venture. In my own experience, starting out as an influencer before social media was widely used was difficult, to say the least.

To help reach my goals, I set myself sound ground rules. For example, I was faithful to the little things and careful with the small amount of money that was coming in. Instead of spending that income on myself, I invested it in recruiting my first employee. She was inexperienced and didn't have a lot of workplace skills, so I made the commitment to train her.

Although I wanted to jump straight into the big events and get out there on stage more often as a speaker, I learned I had to spend time focusing on the small, mundane things, such as teaching my employee all aspects of the business—from checking her emails before she sent them out to encouraging her to use her initiative and ideas. It was only when I was confident that she understood the standards and values of my business that I felt I could refocus on my bigger goals.

Today I have teams operating around the world, including a large one based in the Philippines. It quickly became clear that because the Philippines has a different culture and a different first language from Australia, we needed to spend time with each member of our team there to show them how our company works. We spent time upskilling our colleagues, training them up to the level at which Speakers Institute operates, and sharing with them our approach to our work. This process reminded me that as business leaders we all have to be faithful to the smaller details and eventually the big things will come.

As a manager and leader, I have always made sure that the small jobs were carried out effectively and to a high standard. Across our global organisation, there's not a single role or task that I haven't filled or done myself at some stage. From when I was starting out until today, I have been hands on in developing the processes and systems for our business. From a practical point of view, if your business doesn't have the right structures in place early on, your staff won't know how to move forward, no matter how good they are. Set up strong foundations that people can build on; don't bring in staff and hope they will build these foundation blocks for you, as they might not suit your style or meet your standards.

Build your team and surround yourself with great colleagues you can trust to look after the smaller details. Then you can focus on the big picture.

As Speakers Institute has grown, I've recruited employees with great attitudes, trained them in the way we work, supported them as they learned the company values, and talked with them about our aims and KPIs. Of course, you can't always be sure you've found the right person for your team; not everyone will fit in. But once you have a colleague who is an asset to your growing company, you can gain their respect by showing that you have done their job in the past and know what is involved. The day-to-day operations of running a business are extremely important. So too is the vision that guides the entire enterprise. If you're connected to and in love with that vision, you can influence others with it.

Take the time to talk with your team about your vision for the company, so it becomes their vision too.

Starting out, be ready to spend time on the small, intrinsic tasks — training people, writing manuals, developing procedures and processes, building systems — to help your organisation, your business or your influence to grow.

Who wants to be a millionaire?

When we think big financially, we think of millionaires and billionaires, what they're worth, their assets and cash. It's all about the money. But people's perspectives are changing and the world of influence, and success itself, is no longer based on monetary value, or at least not on that alone. True success is measured by how many people's lives you have impacted and helped change for the better. The new definition of a millionaire is someone who has had a positive impact on more than a million people's lives.

Start small but set standards that will support you as you grow

Every successful entrepreneur knows what it's like to kick off small and to expect trials and missteps on the journey. But when you talk to them about their achievements, many will tell you of the importance of setting ground rules from day one. If your ground rules match your values and the expectations of your clients and audience, you'll be on your way to growing a big, healthy business and having a major impact as a leader and influencer.

Here are 10 ground rules every leader and influencer can usefully refer to.

1. Be a good leader

Be an authentic, committed leader. Show your leadership qualities in everything you do, even if you're working for someone else.

Start by gathering your thoughts. According to Canadian business executive, TV personality, author and politician Kevin O'Leary, you should be able to articulate why you are a leader worth following in 90 seconds or less.

Show the people around you why you are an outstanding leader; show them by example, by what you do.

And make sure you can deliver on your promises. Some of the most successful people in the world got there because they followed through by executing what they said they could do.

2. Be congruent with your brand

Always treat yourself like a brand. Whether at work or in your personal life, perception is everything. Your brand is how you want the world to see you. But it also invites self-reflection, because you need to be aware of how you appear to others. So be congruent with your brand. If your brand shows you as an empathetic leader who is aware of the needs of people around you, for example, then take the time to listen to what people have to say.

3. Learn from your experiences

Good and bad work experiences can influence the way you see difficult situations. Instead of letting bad experiences bring you down, learn from them. Acknowledge that those experiences prepared you for other, even more challenging environments. Then, on your road to success, you can overcome objections and obstacles more confidently; you won't let them stop you.

Those experiences may also help you to find innovative ways to resolve difficulties. Whether it's challenging people or a demanding environment you have to contend with, if you manage the situation well, or you take the time to reflect on what you could have done better, you'll be all the stronger for it.

4. Make meaningful connections

You're going to form connections no matter where you work. You interact with colleagues and clients and form professional relationships. Genuine meaningful connections can generate loyalty from those around you. How do you form meaningful connections? Simply by being genuinely helpful. Making positive contributions through your work and in your personal life will inspire others and will pay off by being reciprocated in the long term.

5. Embrace the spirit of entrepreneurship

Innovation and uniqueness are qualities often found in the most successful entrepreneurs, and no matter what field you're in they can go a long way in furthering your business goals. Always be ready to step back, assess, and think of new ideas and different ways of doing things.

6. Identify your strengths

One of the keys to successful branding is knowing your strengths and playing to them. That includes those strengths and attributes that make you different. You're a unique person with unique advantages and offerings. Work out how you can turn these strengths into something that can help you achieve your goals.

7. Stay focused

When you're starting out, it's easy to get carried away by lots of plans. Try to maintain your focus. This can apply to different areas of your life, but especially when you're working on an idea. You can easily get side-tracked just when your idea starts to gain momentum. Why? Because as billionaire Mark Cuban points out, 'When it gets hard, people start looking for other things to do.' At such times you have to maintain your focus and play to your strengths.

Cuban also reminds us that business success was never meant to be easy. If it were, everyone would be rich and heading up their own company. So, 'When it gets tough, you gotta dig in and work hard.'

8. Transparency is crucial

Transparency is a tool that helps brands to inspire trust. One study showed that people were willing to take the following actions for a transparent brand:

- Switch brands.
- Pay more for the brand.
- Stay loyal for life.

If you offer a service rather than a product, you can interpret this a little differently. Keep in mind that operating honestly and openly helps build a sense of community. Clients feel closer to you when you let them into your process.

9. Know your audience

Who is your audience? When it comes to leading, knowing who's ready to join you is important.

At first, and as an ongoing practice, *do your research*. Get to know your audience on different levels. Who are they demographically, culturally, emotionally? This can help you develop a buyer's persona. Once you have done this, you can grow your business so it offers the products or services your identified audience wants and needs.

10. Know who you are

Why describe yourself in just a few words? Because it helps to clearly define your business. It's easy to get lost in long, convoluted mission descriptions. It's harder to be clear and concise, but it is important. If you can't clearly explain who you are or what you have to offer, your clients, colleagues or audience won't know what to make of you and might simply turn away.

Be genuine and authentic. Know who you are and why you are worth listening to or working with, and don't be shy about sharing this information with others. You will only grow your circle of influence or your business when you can talk with confidence about what you can offer.

IN A NUTSHELL

We all want the big things life has to offer. That's understandable. It's part of our nature, and it's great to be ambitious. Where would the world be if we didn't think big? I'm the first to admit I want big things for my children and for my colleagues. But be prepared to take time and focus on the details when you're starting out. As a leader, don't dismiss someone's concerns because they seem trivial to you. They are clearly important to that person and they are looking to you for help.

Don't rush in and make mistakes when taking your time and assessing the situation could lead to great outcomes.

Make plans and develop structures to expand your sphere of influence. Spend time on building your content and your social media profile; develop your own authentic brand. Talk with your colleagues about your big ideas and listen to them if they want to discuss the details of their work.

It's always true: big things grow from small beginnings.

CHAPTER ELEVEN

WHY
before how

Everyone has a natural genius within them, or at the least knows how to do something really well. You know, those moments when someone comes up to you and says, 'Wow, you make that look so easy. Can you teach me how you do it?' At the same time, most leaders and influencers also have inquiring minds: we want to keep learning and finding out how things work.

Some of us enjoy finding things out for ourselves; others prefer to follow a 'how-to' manual. The desire to learn how is essential if you want to master a new skill and upgrade your expertise.

How is also the question to pose when you are teaching someone a formula or system. You can use 'how to' as the starting point when helping others gain new knowledge. As a thought leader, speaker, influencer and expert, you need a useful, current, teachable framework, which might include your own formula, system or step-by-step guidelines. This way you can pass on your insights, learnings and advice to others while increasing your own expertise and standing out as an influencer. Passing on your teachable framework, your own intellectual property, relies on 'how to'.

How is the first question we ask throughout our lives as learners. This seemed self-evident, until Simon Sinek's 2009 TED talk, 'How great leaders inspire action', turned the idea on its head. In Sinek's 'Golden Circle', he presents three concentric circles, with 'What' in the outside circle, 'How' in the next one, and 'Why' right in the centre. He proposes that it's neither *what* we do nor *how* we do it that is the most important question to ask ourselves. We need to start with our *why*.

People often focus on 'what you need to do and how you need to do it'. What and how are certainly important, but there's a powerful argument for making why your starting point.

Sinek tells us that all companies, no matter their size, start with 'Why'. He explains: 'By "Why" I don't mean to make money, that's always a result. By "Why", I mean what's your purpose, cause or belief? Why does your company exist? Why did you get out of bed this morning? And why should anyone care?'

Everyone wants to make money, and most of us need to. That's a given. But if making money is your only motivator, you'll struggle to build a personal brand or following, or to become a true leader.

You need a purpose to persuade people to care about you, and that's your own distinct why. If you focus only on money, there's nothing to separate you from the crowd. But if you have a cause you really believe in, people are more likely to align themselves with you, which means they're more likely to share your message and it will reach a larger audience.

Ultimately, defining and sharing your why effectively will benefit your business.

Ask yourself why you want to become a speaker, a leader or an influencer. Do you want to inspire others to make positive changes? Do you want to help people avoid mistakes you have made in your life or career? Do you want to help make the world, or your city, town or community, a better place? Do you want to develop a supportive company culture?

Determine for yourself what motivates you, what drives you and persuades people to connect with you — that is your why.

Simon Sinek's TED talk, by the way, is one of the most popular talks on TED.com, with over 50 million views and subtitles in 48 languages. To find out more about his ideas, read his global bestselling book, *Start with Why*.

Little children know to ask why

When my son was in his terrible twos, when he was starting to learn to talk, he would ask, 'But why, Dad?' and 'But why, Mum?' over and over, and about everything. He wasn't asking, 'How do I do it?' or 'What do I do?' He was asking, 'Why?' Like most young kids — like most of us at any age really — he wanted to know why first. Because if we know why, then the what and the how will fall into place.

In my own childhood and teenage years at school, I wasn't overly academic. The traditional education system didn't serve me well, and that was mainly because at school they were telling me, 'This is what you need to do, and this is how you need to do it.' They were using traditional teachings styles that didn't work with a disruptor like me. I had never conformed to the standard conventions that people were expected to follow. I questioned everything, and I mean everything, from 'Why do we sleep at night rather than during the day?' to 'Why do we have three meals a day?' Even with such basic givens that most people take for granted, I wanted to know why and to really understand rather than simply conform.

So the traditional education system didn't work for me. I failed English and Maths, and school in general. I was far more stimulated by the social aspect of school and hanging out with my friends. As a teenager, I started doing things I knew I shouldn't. This led me to disobey my parents. My life didn't follow the straight and narrow path that was expected of me. Before long I was kicked out of school and I never went back, which meant I had to fend for myself.

There I was, unskilled and under-educated in a traditional sense, but I always knew deep down in my soul, in my spirit, that my life had meaning, even though I really wasn't sure what it was, so I felt frustrated. In my own way, as a young man, I tried to find meaning around my why. I had so many questions. Why do I exist? Why do I wake up each morning? Why don't I feel fulfilled? The frustration came from not having any answers. I needed to get clarity on my why so I could answer all the questions that were revolving around in my mind.

I grew so frustrated with having no answers that I decided to do something about it. Instead of just letting life take hold of me, I decided to grab hold of life itself. I started searching. I asked myself, 'What is my place?' and demanded an answer. I asked myself, 'What do I love doing?' Do I want to make a lot of money or work for charity? Do I want to work for corporations or for governments? Do I want to save the planet? I spent a lot of time combing through all these options and trying to work out what goal would offer me true fulfilment.

Eventually, I found my why. I realised that I exist on this planet because I want to help other people. True success, for me, would mean serving and contributing to someone else's life and actually seeing them blossom, seeing them break through. Playing a part in someone else's transformation is what would bring me real fulfilment and joy.

The more I understood my why, the more clarity I felt. Everything I've done in my life — from starting a charity in India and assisting kids living with a disability to working for a job agency helping people get work — has been congruent with my desire to help people. Everything I've done in my working life has revolved around people.

Over time I decided that I could train others to help people as well and to help themselves. I could inspire people who have a similar value system to my own. This is what I do today—and, you know, I'm starting to live my dream. I'm training thousands of people, who in turn train more—and so it spreads. As these people become influencers and work to make a positive difference in the world, the ripple effect can be felt around the globe.

Once I had found what I loved to do, which is help people, I could set out on a path to achieve a true sense of fulfilment. My why is about helping others find their fulfilment. You now know how I found mine.

Today, understanding the why of my organisation helps me to lead and grow my business. I have also come to understand why I do what I do in my personal life—why I get up every morning, why I'm married, why I have kids.

Once I came to understand the why in my professional and personal life, the what and the how started to fall into place. Because when your why is strong and clear, you will find a way to make things happen—you'll find your how and discover what you need to do.

Commander's Intent

As I build my business and take it global, I use a principle called Commander's Intent. It is based on a military formula in which the commanding officer explains to their team why something must be done when they assign a task. The theory, which I have seen work over and over in our business, is that the more your people understand the purpose behind what needs be done—that is, the why—the better they will do it.

Bestselling author Josh Kaufman, who writes about business, entrepreneurship and applied psychology, explains, 'By being clear about the purpose behind a plan, others can act toward that goal without the need of constant communication ... When you communicate the intent behind your plans, you allow the people you work with to intelligently respond to changes as they happen.'

The way I see it, I don't want to micromanage my staff, and equally, people resent having a manager looking over their shoulder all the time. Also, I don't want to employ people who will simply conform, follow an established pathway and never show any initiative. Just as the military wanted their generals and soldiers to think and fend for themselves, as a thought leader, I too want colleagues who will think for themselves. In our business, instead of following a standard manual that sets out what our staff need to do and how they should do it, we also encourage our colleagues to recognise that there's often more than one way to reach an outcome. In some situations you do have to follow a direction, but in others you can find your own way to reach the desired result.

Having said this, I can't afford for anyone in the company to lose sight of our purpose and what we should all be working towards. We all have to understand and share our why. To do this, I start by fully explaining what outcome we're aiming for, what our intention is and where we are going. Then it's up to our staff to find the best way to make it happen. So long as the outcome is clearly articulated and our values, mission and goals are shared, then each person can find their own way to achieve the outcome. They may find different ways to answer the question, 'How?'

We have implemented the Commander's Intent in our leadership structure throughout our business. As more general managers come on board in different countries, and more chief facilitators lead our events, we now base many of our training formulas on outcome, on the why first, before the what and how. In this way, we're creating more leaders within our organisation, rather than people who just follow a standard how-to formula without thinking for themselves.

I believe that when leading a team you should always encourage a discussion of why before you start to talk about how. That way you can begin to motivate everyone, and the team can share ownership of an idea or a goal. It's not about just telling the team, 'This is how you do it,' because ultimately they will ask, 'But why are we doing it this way?'

Don't be afraid if people in the team start questioning the why. It gives you another opportunity to explain it clearly, to clarify what it means to you, and perhaps even to find new ways to approach it.

Keep the why relevant as your business grows

When you're setting up your business, you and the other leaders and your colleagues can collaborate or contribute to creating your vision statement, to defining the why—why the company exists, why we do what we do, why are we unique, and so on. In this initial process of collaboration, everyone has a voice.

As more people join the organisation, take the time to talk with them about the mission statement and the why. Discuss and explain how you initially reached the why and who was involved in its creation. During this process, your new colleagues will buy into that vision. Of course, some companies have such a strong, compelling mission statement and such a clear and relevant why that people are attracted to them for that reason above all others. They know exactly what the company or organisation stands for and want to buy into it and build a career there.

I believe, by the way, that once the vision statement has been created and locked in, it should not change. If anyone in the company believes it should change, then they need to give a very good reason; they need to explain their thoughts clearly and be ready to debate them respectfully with their colleagues. However, there is no point in clinging to your why if it is no longer relevant or if it's holding you back.

Everything in a business should lead to success. Leaders have to continually question and pivot. If your business is not achieving the success you want and the results must be improved, then clearly a pivot is needed. The easiest way to start this process is by assessing the how. How are processes being done? How are people working? Examine and analyse the details and the day-to-day operations. If that isn't enough to achieve the results you need, then step back and examine your why.

The why is at the top of the food chain. It's the big picture. So you'd only change it if it's essential to do so, as it would probably mean also changing the fundamentals of how you work and what you do. But good leaders are open to change and will always be prepared to reassess what they are doing.

As a leader, you know that if the how and what aren't working, you will need to look at the why.

So this is really important: if your company's not successful, and you have started to question the why, then put in place a process for reviewing it. Collaboration is often the best approach.

Work out who should be involved in the process, then create a place of respectful criticism and active listening. Invite everyone around the table to put forward their ideas; give everyone an opportunity to speak and be heard. Follow this with time for questions and discussion. You want everyone at the table to fully understand one another's thoughts about the why.

My suggestion in situations like this is to bring in someone from outside the company to facilitate the conversation to eliminate bias, so people are not only listening to the leader or manager. The facilitator will raise questions such as, 'How can we come up with a general consensus that's going to work for everyone?', 'What's not working?' and 'Where do you want to go?'

Keep in mind that the best facilitators don't tell people what they want to hear. Even though the facilitator probably knows some of these answers, they will not direct people to the formula or how to do something. A great facilitator will ask the right questions in order to draw out everything from the individuals and then come up with a general consensus. So bring in an outstanding facilitator to create a collaborative decision-making process.

Sometimes you need to shine a bright light on your why, when the how and what are no longer really working.

IN A NUTSHELL

We always need to understand the why first. *Why are we doing this?* When we can clearly see the vision and follow the purpose of our why, then we can start to find different ways to achieve it. We can then experiment with the what and how in our organisation or in our own lives.

As a leader, if you want to create other thought leaders within your organisation, don't start by teaching them how to do something or by telling them what they should do. Because then you're encouraging them to conform to one way of doing things. If you want to create true leaders, start by talking with them about *why we do it, why we want to head this way, why we want to achieve this outcome.* Once you ignite the why in your colleagues, then they can start to work out their own ways of achieving it, their own how.

CHAPTER TWELVE

STORY
before data

Data is an anchor. It can give you reliable support and confidence when you're selling or aiming to win people over to your way of thinking. It provides the solid facts and figures needed to back up your claims, and by using data you can present clients and colleagues with tested outcomes that absolutely no one can dispute.

Data is numbers and statistics; it's information you can use to make logical decisions. Understanding and analysing data related to your company or organisation is imperative, both for the company's survival and for it to move forward. With the relevant data and the knowledge of how to use it, you can steer your business in the right direction to become more successful. So data must always be there, front of mind, as an essential strategising and planning tool.

Of course, data's not human based; it's about measurements not emotions. On the other hand, story is all about people; it's about our feelings, experiences and emotions. It's the cornerstone of our emotional decision making when we act according to our instincts, and it always has been.

You know that feeling you get when something makes complete sense; it's logical in every respect, but your gut tells you otherwise so you're not prepared to go ahead? You're deciding about buying or doing something. You're about to take on a big task, and everything makes sense. The numbers add up. You've checked the details and analysed the data; you have all the facts and figures to make an informed decision. But in your gut you're still unsure. Your instinct isn't connected with the possible outcome, so you're not ready to take the next step.

Let's say my wife and I decide to buy a new car. We go to the showroom, and the salesperson comes over and gives us all the information and explains all the features, takes us through all the benefits of the particular vehicle we're looking at and explains why it will be ideal for us. We've also done our own research, and we have a checklist of what we want and need. This car ticks all the boxes, and I'm thinking, *Yep, it's perfect. Let's buy it. It all makes sense.* But if my wife turns to me and says, 'Sam, I'm not feeling it', do you think we're going to buy that car? No way, no chance at all. We're not going to buy it.

Even when we have all the information and the data aligns with what we need, if our gut says no, if our emotions aren't engaged, then we won't jump in and buy that product or service. This means that as leaders, influencing the future of our clients, our colleagues or our company, we must know the data, but we must also connect emotionally.

And the greatest way to inspire emotion within yourself and to influence others is through the power of story.

Story's always going to be our trump card. Whatever your skillset or area of expertise, whatever data and information you can access, I can probably find better services, more relevant information and more highly trained experts offering advice online right now for free.

So your greatest asset, what makes you stand out from the crowd, is actually not your skillset or your expertise. It's your story.

No one else on the planet has your story or your ability to share it. You have something unique to offer to an audience, clients or colleagues. Unlock its power and build your own following based on your experiences and insight.

This means that to be an outstanding leader, you need to be an outstanding story sharer, storyshower, storyteller. You must learn how to share powerful stories to evoke emotions. Yes, data is good — it's essential and it's pivotal to decision making — but story will generally win out over data when you want someone to take out their money and buy.

Types of stories

There are two main types of story to consider. One type is the stories we tell ourselves about ourselves. Many of these are actually our limiting beliefs. They tell us why we're not good enough, why we're not worthy, why we aren't strong leaders. They tell us, 'Hey look, I'm too insecure,' or 'I'm not loved,' or 'I don't belong,' or 'I'm an imposter in this role.' These stories, which form a part of our inner dialogue, don't serve us well. Strong leaders need to clear their minds of such limiting beliefs. Push them away, or get help from others who can squash them with you. They are the negative stories we don't want, because they harness our emotions in ways that pull us down.

The type of stories I want to talk about here are the ones we share with others. They are the narratives that help us connect with others, conveying our views, our experiences and what we can offer them. Human beings are hardwired for stories.

From when we are children all through our adult life, we think in stories and we love to engage with them. Stories have been around since the beginning of time. They have been passed down from our ancestors. The stories we were told by our parents and grandparents probably helped form our beliefs and values. We mightn't know a lot of the data from back in the times of our forebears, but we are still inspired by their stories.

So as leaders, while data is very useful to us, stories are even more important. Think about how you share stories with other people, how you process ideas and concepts through stories, and also how stories trigger your emotions that influence your decision making.

Using stories to grow your business and bring people into your circle

These days, customers want to know an organisation's story around how it began, its values and what it stands for. We also want to know the narrative of a company's services; we want to follow the supply chain of its products and to do this we need to hear their story. Were the products produced ethically? Where were they made, who made them and in what were their working conditions? When making a major purchase, we no longer just look at the price and the specifications — the data. We want to be convinced that what we are buying is good for the planet and for the producers, as well as suiting our own needs. Our emotions come into play in our decision making every day.

The bottom line now is that if you're trying to sell me the best product but I don't like the story of that product, or if I can't find out its story, I'm not going to take out my wallet. Let's say you have a pretty good product; it's clearly not the best, but it's pretty good. And you are prepared to share its story, so I can discover where it was made, who made it, and how it matches my values. If you can give me a story that will engage my emotions as well as my brain, then that's when I'll take out my wallet and buy it.

An organisation with a strong, transparent and authentic story will always trump one that has a great product but doesn't share its story.

Sincerely sharing a story will attract both buyers and others in the marketplace and the highest calibre of staff. The generation now entering the workforce expect a business to have a good story to share and a commitment to its staff and clients, as well as to the community. Many young people are looking to work for an organisation that is socially responsible and engaged, rather than a disengaged organisation that pays well. They want to join a company that is smart, that analyses the data, but more importantly, they want an emotional connection with the managers, the company's leaders and its products.

Control your own story

David Brier is a well-recognised branding expert who has won hundreds of awards for his work with various companies. He's also the bestselling author of *Brand Intervention: 33 Steps to Transform the Brand You Have into the Brand You Need.* Brier talks of how you need to maintain control over your own story: 'If you don't give the market the story to talk about, they'll define your brand's story for you.'

It's simple yet powerful advice. Nobody can talk about your story, who you are or what you stand for better than you. Many new influencers allow market forces to guide them. Instead of creating their own niche with their story, they try to fit into a standard mould that they think consumers want. This means their customers dictate their story. And when that happens, you have no chance of being authentic. You're selling a message that isn't your own.

Stay in control of your own story. Others may help you to refine it, but make sure you determine how your story goes and how you share it.

Stories aren't all about the hard sell

Through his story, entrepreneur Gary V (Gary Vaynerchuk) is one of the most in-demand speakers in the world. He's the CEO of VaynerMedia, an advertising agency servicing Fortune 100 clients. He has also published five bestselling books and built an empire around his ability to engage an audience. Gary V is a storyshower. It's how he has managed to stay relevant as the internet and the tools available to him have evolved. To read more about his personal story, visit www.garyvaynerchuk.com.

Many salespeople, speakers and managers jump straight into their hard sells. They tell people what they have to offer then try to get them to buy into it. More often than not, this approach doesn't work. Consumers have evolved over the years. Today we want people to show us something that engages us, that connects with us on an emotional level, before we come close to making our purchasing decision.

'I'm building for the long term because I think it's about the brand,' Gary says. 'So many of you are in it for the quick sale, and you are going to be forgotten.'

Hard selling your virtues is tantamount to hard selling a product. You may get a couple of people to buy into it in the short term. But the message has no substance. Eventually, you alienate the audience and they no longer connect with you. Gary has built up his personal brand and is never anything less than authentic; he shows people what he stands for. If you're constantly having to *tell* people who you are and what you stand for, you're not doing a good enough job of *showing* them. You need to show through your stories who you are, what is important to you and what you can offer others.

You create a deeper connection if you can convey your values to the audience, your clients or your colleagues through your stories and actions.

It comes down to the crucial point of being yourself. You don't have to be a natural seller to share a story. Trying to force the hard sell, be it of a product or of your personality, comes off as inauthentic.

Instead, be a storyshower who connects with your customers. The selling part comes naturally once you're working with an engaged client. Then you can present them with the data.

Take inspiration from other leaders, but don't rely on their stories—build your own. Identify your strengths to find out what makes you, your organisation or your product unique. Show people your story instead of constantly going for the hard sell. And be prepared to break down your own walls so you can show people the true emotions behind your stories.

As an international speaker, Gary V points to listening to your audience as one of the keys to creating your personal brand and following. They're the people who have already connected with you. Answer their questions and tell them stories that inspire them. If they're satisfied, they'll connect with you, they'll come back to hear more from you and they'll often share your stories with likeminded people. Hit them with lots of data and figures and statistics and many will turn off, even if they were really hoping to build a connection with you or with what you had to offer.

Balance your emotional content

How successfully you share your story comes down to emotion. But it's not as simple as it sounds. Balancing your emotional content is the key to showing people a story they will engage with.

My career as a speaker started with a life-threatening car crash. On my road to recovery, I realised that my story could influence and inspire others. But my first paid speaking engagement didn't go as I'd expected. After capturing the audience's attention with a few jokes and some statistics, I moved on to telling my story. I didn't pause for breath. I just kept going without giving the audience any chance to absorb the emotional weight of what I was saying.

Worse still, I showed no vulnerability. Instead of showing people how devastating the accident was for me and for Kate, I cracked jokes, over and over. I put up barriers that made it impossible for my audience to connect. I knew that humour has a place in connecting with an audience and can elicit joyful emotions, but now I realise that humour isn't something you should sprinkle through a story about a tragic accident. In that moment, up on stage, I learned the importance of balancing my emotional content. I discovered that I had to show my true emotions and how I really felt about what had happened.

Vulnerability makes you authentic and keeps your clients, colleagues or audience engaged. But you must balance your emotional content.

If you're sharing a difficult experience, let them feel it. If you're explaining how, when you were starting out, your company went through some tough times and you didn't know if you could keep going, then let them feel what you were feeling then. People want to go on an emotional ride with a storyshower and know that the story you are sharing is authentic.

On the flipside, don't dwell on vulnerability. That could make you seem self-pitying. Understand the emotion behind every aspect of your story, and show it.

Five keys to storytelling

Great stories can lead your audience, clients and customers towards thoughtful reflection through which they see themselves and their world in new ways. Your story will appeal to their emotions, memories and imagination, and have a unique power to make a meaningful impact on those you share it with.

Here are some tips to help you share your story:

Identify and understand the outcome you are aiming for.

Your story needs to have a clear outcome for your listeners. It has to have a purpose and to make a point. Always keep in mind what you want the audience to take away. Understanding the outcome you are aiming for allows you to craft engaging stories based on compelling messages that people want to hear about.

Share a story that is interesting, meaningful and engaging.

No matter how significant your message, you can't share it with your listeners effectively unless you give them a reason to care about what you have to say. You have to catch their attention by talking about something *they* are interested in. Keep them on the edge of their seats, and engage their hearts and minds.

Build tension and anticipation.

Make your listeners wonder what will happen next. Will things turn out all right? Will the problem — and perhaps by extension their problem — be resolved? To build tension, you can introduce a challenge early on. The audience's curiosity as to the outcome will increase their anticipation and desire to find out what happens next.

Connect with each person in the room so they connect with you.

Offer the listener a chance to see themselves in your story. The more the audience is involved in your story, the more memorable and valuable your message becomes.

Let the listener step into your story and remember it.

A good way to convey your message is to trigger a memory and raise a familiar, shared experience. This connects your listeners' own lives to the story, making it more memorable.

By addressing these five points, you give your listeners the opportunity to change their perceptions, which can help to inspire positive change.

IN A NUTSHELL

We can't do business without data. We'd fumble around and never make informed decisions if we didn't learn from what has happened before and assemble the facts to support the expected outcomes. There's no question that collecting, analysing and using data is essential in every field.

Before data, however, come stories. Most of us want to make emotional connections with others; for better or worse, we think with our hearts as well as our brains, and there's nothing better than a story to create these emotional ties. We might not be able to access all the data from hundreds of years ago, but we still have the stories from that time. Why? Because stories are hardwired in our brains. We heard them when we were little kids and we still love to hear them now. So before we buy products and services, and before we are prepared to follow leaders, we need to hear their authentic stories.

BOUNCE FORWARD

When you need to make sense of the big things in life, it can help to use a metaphor. Consider the people and experiences that have shaped your world and use them to develop your metaphor, your story.

My story? Squeezed around the dinner table with my parents and 10 brothers and sisters, who were my inspiration, my influencers, the people who made me ask questions and consider my purpose. As I first outlined in the introduction and built on through this book, that became a powerful metaphor for me when thinking about leadership and influence, and the attitudes, beliefs and strengths that would be of greatest positive value for me. Even now I can look around at the 12 seated with me at the table and abstract, difficult concepts become real and resolvable.

I have shared with you the 12 seats at my table. Who will sit at your table? Who will you invite and who will you avoid? With only 12 places, consider how you will prioritise. As you become a leader and influencer, consider who and what will offer the most value in helping you to create the strong foundations on which to build your legacy.

Many years ago, as I related in chapter 8, I developed the concept I call *Bounce Forward*. In essence, this is about using and learning from a crisis, or the tough stuff in life, to Bounce Forward into the best possible place and mindset to propel you successfully into the future.

For a hundred years we haven't experienced a crisis — medical, economic, social or psychological — to rival what we have faced in 2020, as we navigated our isolation and our fears. We have learned the hard way the impact a single tiny invisible virus can have on human civilisation. Coming out of this time of crisis, we have to learn how not simply to pivot, but in many ways to reinvent our way of life, our businesses and even our mission in order to find our place in this new world.

During the COVID-19 pandemic, we have seen that the nations and leaders who had built solid foundations were the ones who navigated their countries through the crisis most successfully. People were prepared to trust and follow them. We need to hold on to our vision and values, or be prepared to reassess them. We must have the right foundations to successfully innovate through the tough times.

I encourage you to invest in your foundations and ensure that you have the right seats at the table to help you navigate any crises, whether personal or professional, you may find yourself facing.

When you have chosen your 12, listen to them, rely on them, then look outward and ask, 'What do people need?' 'What can I offer?' 'How can I serve them and keep them safe?' Then you'll be a leader people will follow.

INDEX

Printed in Australia
06 Apr 2021
761405